KITCHEN

REMODELING

Assess Needs and Wishes Kitchen

Design and Planning

NOELLE GILL

Legal & Disclaimer

The information contained in this book and its contents is not designed to replace or take the place of any form of medical or professional advice. It is not meant to replace the need for independent medical, financial, legal, or other professional advice or services, as may be required. The content and information have been provided for educational and entertainment purposes only.

This book's content and information have been compiled from reliable sources, and it is accurate to the best of the Author's knowledge, information, and belief. However, the author cannot guarantee its accuracy and validity and cannot be held liable for any errors and/or omissions. Further, changes are periodically made to this book as and when needed. Where appropriate and/or necessary, you must consult a professional (including but not limited to your doctor, attorney, financial advisor, or such other professional advisor) before using any of the suggested remedies, techniques, or information in this book.

i

Upon using the contents and information contained in this book, you agree to hold harmless the Author from and against any damages, costs, and expenses, including any legal fees potentially resulting from the application of any of the information provided by this book. This disclaimer applies to any loss, damages, or injury caused by the use and application, whether directly or indirectly, of any advice or information presented, whether for breach of contract, tort, negligence, personal injury, criminal intent, or under any other cause of action. You agree to accept all risks of using the information presented in this book.

TABLE OF CONTENTS

———— ◆◇◆ ————

HOW TO RENOVATE A KITCHEN: IDEAS, COSTS, AND ADVICE

——— ◆◇◆ ———

A high-quality kitchen, as far as the furniture is concerned, can last in good condition even for 20 or 30 years; having said that, on the other hand, appliances not only have a much shorter useful life but, over time, they become "obsolete" and then. However, our kitchen is still in excellent condition, it is quite natural that after ten or fifteen years, visually (and sometimes not only!), it does not satisfy us more fully, because the tastes and trends in furniture now change from year to year, as well as lifestyle habits change.

Therefore, the desire to renovate the rooms of the house is understandable, especially if it is a place like a kitchen, which is, in fact, one of the most vital and used spaces in a house. It is intimate and familiar, the one to which we associate the idea of "home" more than any other, also by virtue of the scents and memories it arouses in each of us.

If, therefore, you have decided in one way or another that it is time to review the layout of your kitchen, read our tips to do it in the best way because, even if it does not seem but, then there are many things to decide and the practical and aesthetic implications are innumerable, so it is good to carefully consider each choice, so as not to regret it, at least for the next 15-20 years.

Furthermore, it is not said that it is necessary to spend a fortune to bring a breath of fresh air; if you want a total revolution, you will have to be willing to spend and take on the inconvenience that construction work entails inside an inhabited house. However, sometimes by spending reasonable amounts, you can still get the desired result; let's see how.

Family kitchen (How to renovate a kitchen: ideas, costs, and advice)

First step: carry out a survey and focus on studying the space. When you want to intervene, the very first thing to do is a precise and detailed survey of the environments you want to renovate to be able to give everything back graphically. You can also survey by yourself, using a meter or, better still, a "disto," that is a laser pointer that is used to measure distances; the important thing is to accurately and correctly mark the presence of any windows or doors with their sense of opening, as well as that of niches or protrusions and then record the position in which the gas and water connections are located, the discharge of the latter and all the so-called "power sockets," i.e., those power sockets dedicated to the most powerful appliances, light sockets, and light points.

By putting all this information together, you will understand how you would like to distribute the various elements in space and if this is feasible, and at what price. Because if you want to change the existing layout, in some cases radically, it is pretty simple as it is enough to make traces on the wall to reposition and adapt the systems; other times, it may be essential to remove the existing flooring to make traces in the screed. But, again, this is because work is feasible but more expensive and time-consuming.

Attention then, because often today, unlike what happened in the past, when we talk about the kitchen, we refer not to a closed and independent environment but rather to a portion of space open to the living room, the so-called kitchenette, and this too can lead to some more problems because it is also necessary to relate to functions and furnishings that go beyond the kitchen itself.

Second step: understand how much you can spend and how much you want to intervene. Once you are aware of what theoretically could be achieved in the spaces available, the time comes to collide with the reality of the facts and establish a budget to devote to the kitchen renovation: only in this way will you be able to understand how and in what measure you should intervene. For example, it is useless to delude yourself into buying a new kitchen with a central island if you have a few thousand euros available; it will be better to seek a compromise so that the final result is as close to the desired one.

If we have no particular problems, the simplest solution is obviously to change everything: scrap the old kitchen and replace it with a new one complete with the latest generation appliances, perhaps also laying new floors and a new wall covering. So let's see how to do this in these cases, but then let's try to understand what can be done as an alternative if you want to limit expenses.

HOW TO CHOOSE
THE RIGHT TILES
FOR YOUR KITCHEN

————— ◆◇◆ —————

One of the most popular rooms in the house has always been the kitchen area. In recent years, space has become multipurpose: from a place in charge of meals to an environment to live, share, and dialogue. Because if it is true that the average time spent in the kitchen decreases from year to year, it is equally valid that a beautiful kitchen becomes the perfect place to relax in front of a glass of wine after a day at work.

Due to their intrinsic technical characteristics, they do not absorb liquids; they are easy to clean and antibacterial as well as aesthetic they allow infinite combinations also; thanks to the perfect slabs for wall coverings on the tops, they have found one of the places in the kitchen of maximum design expression.

Kitchen tiles: tips for laying

If you want to create perfect kitchen coverings using porcelain stoneware, it is essential to devote due care to the installation. To understand how to put tiles in the kitchen, careful planning is required. Getting support from a studio or an interior designer can be useful to understand better what the final result will be. However, it is equally important to discuss with those who will take care of the installation to prevent any critical issues. By correctly following the instructions on laying the tiles in the kitchen, the result will be a homogeneous, precise, easy to clean and maintain over time coating.

One of the most frequently asked questions is undoubtedly how to calculate the right tile height for the kitchen without wall units. Obviously, the answer is not unique but depends on the spaces and effects chosen; however, the absence of wall units allows much more freedom in choosing formats and installation.

The tiles for a modern kitchen

To follow the 2020 trends, the choice falls on tiles for a modern kitchen. For this reason, it is useful to apply a very current and refined coating. To be trendy, we can consider the tiles with a glossy surface, very light and lively colors, and particular shapes and patterns (with a sharp angle and narrower joint). The kitchen environment leaves room for furniture and all the furnishings: the covering must enhance the room, not be the protagonist. It is trendy to find yourself in a smart, minimal but at the same time warm and welcoming kitchen, perfect for spending time there.

The modern style in the kitchen can be associated with the black color; one of the 2020 trends is precisely that of choosing very dark furniture for the decor: in this case, the coverings and the flooring can fall on light but warm colors at the same time, to go in contrast but without ever breaking the harmony of the tones.

Design materials to cover the walls of your kitchen

To have a kitchen in step with the times and trends, it is always necessary to do research. The first step is the choice of the most suitable materials: they must be designed, refined, original, and functional.

Some examples are double-fired tiles, laminate panels, epoxy resin, self-adhesive tiles, and porcelain stoneware. In glossy or opaque white color, the former, perhaps combined with wood, evokes a retro atmosphere, almost from other times. The disadvantage is the possible infiltration of water. On the other hand, the laminate gives an essential result to the space; it is a resistant and easily washable material, especially for professional kitchens.

Its minus is perhaps the compromise with elegance. Although the self-adhesive tiles for the kitchen are characterized by ease of installation and the varied possibility of choice, they are perfect for creating refined and modern environments, whatever the style and genre: the adhesive tiles are suitable for covering many surfaces. Their undoubted disadvantage is the shorter duration. Thanks to their clean and minimal style, epoxy resins have enjoyed great success in recent years. However, pay attention to cracks, which can develop, especially if the installation takes place on a surface that is not perfectly level.

Finally, porcelain stoneware is one of the most requested and chosen materials for the kitchen cladding: especially the use of large slabs allows elegant solutions without compromising functional aspects. Thanks to the intrinsic characteristics of stoneware (resistant, antibacterial, anti-absorption), especially when combined with the absence of joints made possible by large sizes. All these coatings and these tiles for the kitchen have variable prices with a range that ranges from economical solutions to other more exclusive ones.

Tradition: majolica tiles

A truly traditional and timeless alternative for kitchen coverings is majolica tiles: a style where freshness, innovation, modernity, and design meet. The majolica effect of porcelain stoneware is perfect for unleashing the imagination in furnishings and generating trendy combinations, ideal for designing an environment with a unique style. This stoneware effect is an evolution of the floor seen in a much more modern and contemporary way.

The majolica effect tiles for kitchen coverings are the right compromise between elegance and panache; they give the whole environment unique modernity and illuminate the spaces with interesting chiaroscuro. The sheen and richness of the material of this style are excellent for covering the kitchen top with tiles with an essential character but rich in details: this is how the minimal design is transformed into an absolutely trendy design.

Simplicity: porcelain stoneware tiles

When it comes to tiles for a modern kitchen, all the porcelain stoneware collections are an excellent solution: they combine simplicity and a wide range of choices. Porcelain stoneware coverings range from floral designs to geometric patterns, up to the various effects: wood, stone, concrete, metal, paper, bricks, and many others.

An example of porcelain stoneware cladding for a modern kitchen is Be-Square by Emilceramica. The collection celebrates the most essential and pure aspect of concrete, a neutral material with great impact, versatile and timeless, that manages to be the protagonist of the space in a discreet, rigorous, and elegant way. The collection is embellished with a mix of 9 decorated 20x20 cement tiles, with nuances balanced in their intensity and a mix of 20x20 majolica tiles characterized by a material surface with matt and glossy contrasts.

The style: kitchen coverings in marble

Speaking of design, we also speak of style with an elegant and unique kitchen cladding such as marble, one of the most beautiful, noble, and durable materials that embellish any environment. The flooring is enriched by a unique architectural strength given by the marble. The finishes are elegant and very decorative, bright and natural, creating pleasant sensations of refinement and essentiality: completely noble essentiality, which only this material can give to the rooms.

The design leaves room for classicism and preciousness; the space is filled with shades given by unusual and dynamic lights. To give life and shape to kitchen coverings, the answer for stoneware is the marble effect is ideal. Cheaper and now identical to natural stone, it plays down the more classic effect of the surface by generating a very strong aesthetic impact. The keywords for kitchen furnishings are elegance, light, and grace, which is why the choice falls on this effect.

Not just tiles: textured coatings

There are also textured coatings to decorate and furnish the kitchen, not just tiles. Although the textures are three-dimensional coatings that decorate entire design projects, they manage to define the surface thanks to their chiaroscuro effects.

The textures used for the kitchen coverings have geometric, optical, and very abstract shapes, giving the environment a modern and completely innovative character compared to the more classic coverings. Among the latest novelties in textures, the three-dimensionality of the curvilinear motifs stands out, giving the wall completely natural energy.

Kitchen tiles: cleaning tips

After going through the various design and engineering trends, let's also talk about how to clean kitchen tiles. First of all, it is useful to collect all the deposited dust; then, it is recommended to prepare a bucket of boiling water with a glass of white vinegar and a spoonful of baking soda. To give the solution a good scent, choose whether to add a few drops of eucalyptus or citrus fragrance. To thoroughly clean the tiles and the floor, it may be useful to wipe this solution a couple of times. Vinegar is a natural antibacterial, and bicarbonate can remove even the most persistent dirt from coatings and tiles.

Another fundamental issue is cleaning the joints between the kitchen tiles; the solution with vinegar and baking soda is perfect. It can also be useful to add a powerful degreaser that acts on the most persistent dirt and uses an old toothbrush to scrub and get inside the smallest spaces.

PROJECT FOR THE KITCHEN

———— ◆◇◆ ————

The kitchen environment project requires the help of a designer and a furniture shop or a craftsman. He is the first point of contact because he knows the spaces and can think of them according to your needs and the room's shape.

The latter because they know all the solutions and possibilities perfectly, always being able to find a winning solution for you. However, you must know the solutions on the market and have guidelines to choose the perfect kitchen for you, your needs, and your home. The kitchen environment is a microcosm in itself, a bit like the bathroom. Obviously, these are the two spaces in the house where, in addition to aesthetics, all the systems also count. It goes without saying that they certainly need more attention.

When you renovate your home, the kitchen must already be chosen and thought about in the design phase, that is, on paper. The systems must be set up according to the furnishing project; the two things must go hand in hand.

However, the position of the gas, water, and electricity connections are designed, and then, when the work is almost finished, the kitchen is bought. But at this stage, the choice will never be completely free because, how and in any case, you will be linked to the position of the implants, and you will have to adapt.

So the first piece of advice I will give you is:

- Define your needs and your desires. Then, think of the kitchen in the design phase, at least regarding the modularity, arrangement, and type of individual elements (hob, sink, dishwasher, oven, fridge, etc.).

- I'll give you an example. If you want an island sink, you will have to decide on the design because you will have to prepare the water connections exactly where you want the sink. If they have been set up on the wall, you will no longer be able to do anything about them except demolish and redo.

- Now let's move on to the things to know and know and then arrive at a targeted choice sewn on you.
- It will seem clearer to you what it means to design a kitchen.

The following is a simple list.

- Layout: The furniture's dimensions and modularity (island, peninsula, wall units, etc.), ergonomics, the study of paths and handling.
- Materials available for kitchen core and doors, choice of top and worktop
- Choice of hob and hood
- Washing area, sink, and taps
- Essential and non-essential appliances
- Preparation of the interior of the kitchen (columns, baskets, corner solutions, pantries)
- Lighting

FLOORS OF THE MODERN KITCHEN

———— ◆◇◆ ————

How do you identify a modern kitchen? The first relates to the functions that a modern kitchen must perform to meet the needs of those who use it. This means, for example, that the kitchen will be equipped with appliances that meet the needs of contemporary life and with suitable materials for floors, furnishings, and coverings.

Modern kitchen, however, also means kitchen with a modern style, a style characterized by rigorous lines, essential furnishings, trendy colors, and solutions that combine aesthetics and ease of use. These are, for example, easily washable surfaces, resistant to use, and which, over time, maintain a clean, tidy, and new appearance.

The kitchen is a technical environment and is subjected to a more invasive use than the other rooms in the house. This is why the materials used for both the furnishings and the floors and walls must be able to withstand this intense use without being damaged by it and maintaining their characteristics over time.

Modern kitchen with large white stone effect floor

The modern kitchen floor is practical and trendy at the same time. Therefore, the kitchen is modern from an aesthetic and a functional point of view. This particularly concerns floors that will be subjected to persistent trampling, falling of food, and various liquids and therefore must preferably be made of a resistant material.

One of the preferred materials for kitchen floors is porcelain stoneware, which combines excellent durability and resistance with an extremely versatile aesthetic since porcelain stoneware can take on numerous aspects and finishes.

Furthermore, it comes in formats of various sizes that allow you to create different effects, with greater visual continuity or geometric compositions and, again, combinations of tiles of different sizes. For all these reasons, it is also the ideal choice, for example, in the design of an open space containing the kitchen, dining area, and living room inside: three areas with different functions for which the floor can become an interesting element stylistic continuity. So let's see some possible solutions, ideal for a modern and contemporary kitchen from the point of view of design and functions.

Natural oak wood effect floor

Concrete effect porcelain stoneware with an industrial mood. Among the trendiest finishes at the moment, there is concrete-effect porcelain stoneware. This material is characterized by a texture reminiscent of classic concrete but has a smoother surface and is more easily manageable from maintenance. In addition, while the concrete itself can crack, the porcelain stoneware remains unchanged over time.

This type of flooring is available in different colors: shades of gray, the color typically associated with concrete; lighter colors, tending to beige or white, for brighter environments; dark tones, such as anthracite or even black, for more scenographic effects.

In all cases, the concrete-effect porcelain stoneware gives the modern kitchen an industrial and sophisticated style at the same time. Another important aspect of this material is its versatility due to its neutral colors: it easily combines with furniture of different types and colors. A few examples? Concrete-effect porcelain stoneware in light tones is an ideal solution for kitchens. It is necessary to maximize light: perfect in combination with white and light wood; it also lends itself to interesting contrasting color solutions. The darker concrete-effect porcelain stoneware, on the other hand, recalls a more industrial mood and goes well with iron and raw wood furnishings. For an optimal concrete effect, the advice is to minimize the width of the joints to give a greater sense of visual continuity.

Modern kitchen floor with gray concrete effect

Marble-effect porcelain stoneware for a refined style kitchen. Marble is a material that, more than others, evokes elegance and prestige. This is why those who want a refined style for their kitchen can use floors whose surface reproduces the aesthetics of marble with its characteristic veins.

If marble is not recommended in a technical environment such as the kitchen, the floors that reproduce its appearance are an excellent solution while at the same time guaranteeing more advanced technical performance suitable for the kitchen. In the many available variants, the marble-effect porcelain stoneware is an excellent solution: the Carrara marble effect is one of the most popular because it is a classic and has a luminous appearance.

It is elegant and informal at the same time and goes well with sophisticated, classic, contemporary, and even vintage furnishings. In addition, the black marble effect, for example, the marquina, of an intense black with white veins, has a more contemporary and characterful look, which makes it ideal for kitchens open to a glamorous and design-oriented living area.

Modern marble kitchen floor with glossy effect

Kitchen and living room: ultra-modern and super-sophisticated, highly polished and elegant black marble-effect stoneware. Stone effect porcelain stoneware, rustic and contemporary.

In a kitchen with a rustic-chic style, where the atmosphere is informal but sophisticated, the stone-effect porcelain stoneware floor is very suitable. However, being porous and more delicate, real stone is not suitable for technical environments such as the kitchen.

This is why it is advisable to focus on a material such as porcelain stoneware that has excellent performance and at the same time perfectly reproduces the texture of the stone in all its shades: from those that turn towards beige to those that turn towards light gray, from bright white to more intense shades of black. Moreover, the stone-effect porcelain stoneware comes not only in various shades but also in various formats with which you can create interesting combinations between floor and wall covering.

Brownstone effect floor

1. Wood-effect flooring in a modern kitchen? The solution is porcelain stoneware.

2. Are wooden floors a suitable solution for modern kitchens? Unfortunately, it is not entirely because it is a delicate material that stains irreparably and requires specific cleaning and maintenance precautions.

3. The perfect compromise is wood-effect porcelain stoneware that perfectly reproduces the aesthetics of wood but not its delicacy. Porcelain stoneware comes in numerous variations that correspond to the many types of wood normally used for floors and are divided into formats.

4. If marble is not recommended in a technical environment such as the kitchen, the floors that reproduce its appearance are an excellent solution while at the same time guaranteeing more advanced technical performance suitable for the kitchen. In the many available variants, the marble-effect porcelain stoneware is an excellent solution: the Carrara marble effect is one of the most popular because it is a classic and has a luminous appearance.

5. It is elegant and informal and goes well with sophisticated, classic, contemporary, and even vintage furniture. In addition, the black marble effect, for example, the Marquina, of an intense black veined with white, has a more contemporary look and character, which makes it ideal for kitchens open to a glamorous and designer living space.

Modern marble kitchen floor with glossy effect

Kitchen and living room: ultra-modern and super-sophisticated, highly polished and elegant black marble-effect stoneware. Stone effect porcelain stoneware, rustic and contemporary

In a kitchen with a rustic-chic style, where the atmosphere is informal but sophisticated, the stone-effect porcelain stoneware floor is very suitable. However, being porous and more delicate, real stone is not suitable for technical environments such as the kitchen.

This is why it is advisable to focus on a material such as porcelain stoneware that has excellent performance and at the same time perfectly reproduces the texture of the stone in all its shades: from those that turn towards beige to those that turn towards light gray, from bright white to more intense shades of black. Moreover, the stone-effect porcelain stoneware comes not only in various shades but also in various formats with which you can create interesting combinations between floor and wall covering.

Brown stone effect floor

Wood-effect flooring in a modern kitchen? The solution is porcelain stoneware. Are wooden floors a suitable solution for modern kitchens? It is not entirely precisely because it is a delicate material that stains irreparably and requires some specific cleaning and maintenance precautions.

The perfect compromise is wood-effect porcelain stoneware that perfectly reproduces the aesthetics of wood but not its delicacy. Porcelain stoneware comes in numerous variations that correspond to the many types of wood normally used for floors and are divided into formats.

WHAT CAN NOT BE MISSING IN THE KITCHEN

————— ◆◇◆ —————

While remaining faithful supporters of decluttering and rooms free from superfluous objects, we know that some objects in the kitchen are almost fundamental, especially if it is a well-lived room in the house and if those who live there have a passion for good food and company. Let's start by starting with the essential items that cannot be missing from the first days in a new kitchen:

- Potholders / Oven mitt
- Chair cushions
- Non-slip mat for sinks and stoves
- Gas lighter (if necessary)
- Toilet paper

- Films for food
- Hand towels
- Waste bin
- Various detergents and detergents (if you are interested in ecological cleaning, take a look here)

What you need in the kitchen: 2

Obviously, everyone has very different needs, and a great cooking enthusiast may notice the absence of many accessories, but broadly speaking, in the kitchen, they should not be missing:

- Crockery
- A set of dishes for everyday use
- Glasses
- Silverware
- Deep pan (for cooking pasta, for example)
- Multi-purpose pan / Wok
- Small saucepan
- Ladles
- Colander
- Plastic salad bowl/bowls
- Tea/coffee cups
- Dessert bowls

- what to buy for the kitchen

Recommended

- Plate
- Kitchen scale
- Containers for leftovers
- Bottle opener
- Chopping board
- Spatulas
- Rolling pin
- Grater
- Salt & pepper holder / cruet
- Kettle
- Salad spinner
- Colander
- Funnels
- Divider for the cutlery drawer
- Jars

What you need in the kitchen: 4

- Domestic appliances
- Dishwasher
- Blender / Minipimer / Mixer
- Coffee machine

- Optional appliances
- Bread maker
- Fryer
- Smoothie maker
- Kitchen robot
- Toaster

What you need in the kitchen: 1

- For the oven
- Oven gloves
- Trays of various sizes / Cake pan
- Baking molds

98 TRICKS FOR ORGANIZING THE KITCHEN

———— ◆◇◆ ————

The kitchen must be tidy, organized, and functional. So how to reach the goal? Here are 98 practical tips! Everyone in the editorial office has given their contribution because there are things that, to some, seem obvious and banal but that, for someone else, on the other hand, are Columbus's egg. In short, there is always something to learn!

1) What you use several times every day goes into compartments that you can open without bending or with little effort.

2) Things you rarely use can fit on higher shelves or identical wooden or plastic baskets or containers on top of wall cabinets.

3) If you have a base with 4 or 5 drawers, use the upper ones for kitchen cutlery, knives, pelucchino, peeler, scissors, graters, and mandolin.

4) The medium and low drawers are tablecloths or placemats and napkins for daily use.

5) Keep the wooden spoons exposed in a spoon holder or the drawer closest to the burners.

6) Keep knives hanging from a magnetic bar or tucked into a stump.

7) Keep the ladles hanging from a bar or in the first or second drawer.

8) If you keep knives in drawers, always use the blade cover to avoid cutting yourself and preserve the blade's edge.

9) The oil you use for cooking can be visible in a bottle next to the stove or on a shelf immediately above.

10) The reserve oil must be stored in a cool and dark place; near the work surface, keep only one bottle for daily use.

11) Keep a jar of coarse salt and a jar of acceptable salt next to the burners or on the shelf above the hood.

12) Keep coarse salt and fine salt in containers that are easy to open with one hand: cooking will be more

convenient, and if you have dirty hands, you need to touch them with a minimal gesture.

13) Avoid creating heterogeneous drawers or cabinets where it is difficult to find things and keep them in order.

14) Do not mix knives and sharp objects with spoons and tools without blades in the same drawer.

15) Create drawers with homogeneous utensils: it will be easier to find them when you need them and put them away after you have washed them.

16) If you are forced to put wooden spoons, ladles, and sharp objects in the same drawer, separate them with a divider.

17) Divide the glass refrigerator containers from the plastic ones.

18) For plastic containers, you can save space as follows: stack the containers in order of size, insert them one inside the other, and group the lids together, which you can keep vertically stuck in one of the containers.

19) If you have special tools such as pineapple peeler, corer, stoner, meatball tongs, milk frother, etc., you can group them in a box or vase to keep on view.

20) Keep cups, small cups, dessert plates, and fruit bowls close together: they are often used together, making it easier for you to set and serve on the table.

21) In the cabinet under the sink, divide and group the detergents by type of use: dishwashers, degreasers, glass, steel.

22) Order the pantry like the wardrobe: you wouldn't put shoes and T-shirts together, right? Use a similar criterion and divide the foods by type as well

23) REDUCE DISTANCES, i.e., put the tools as close as possible to the work area where you are using them.

24) The compartment or basket containing dishes and glasses must be close to the dishwasher: you need to make minimal movements to empty it.

25) Pots and pans go to the baskets or cabinets closest to the stove.

26) Put the heavier pans in the top basket, making it less tiring to lift and take them out.

27) Separate the pans with cloth, felt, or cardboard 'pan protectors' (you can buy them or make them yourself): you will avoid damaging them, and you can put them back in order more quickly without paying excessive attention to bumps.

28) Colander and salad spinner can be placed in a cabinet near the sink.

29) Dishes and glasses go into the basket or cupboard closest to the dishwasher.

30) The tea towels must be visible and easy to grasp.

31) If you have a large kitchen, but more than one hook for the dish towels, one near the sink, the stove, or the work area.

32) Keep the cutting boards close to the work area and hang them on the wall or vertically inside a base or wall unit.

33) Keep the spices near the stove, preferably insight: it will come to mind more easily to use them.

34) Organize the spices according to the use you make of them: the ones you use most often keep them close at hand, while the more particular ones can stay at the bottom. If you always use many of them, put them in alphabetical order.

35) Spices look better in glass than in plastic containers. You can use glass jars for the group on a shelf inside a door.

36) If you frequently use an aromatic herb, keep a jar on the work surface; it will always allow you to have a few fresh leaves.

37) If you don't have aromatic plants, keep the fresh herbs you buy (basil, rosemary, parsley) in a jar with water near the worktop.

38) If you cannot keep small appliances in sight, dedicate a base to them and apply a pull-out basket in the lower part to leave the necessary height. You can group blender, food processor, centrifuge, planetary mixer, etc. At the top, you will have space for a shelf or another removable compartment for their accessories

39) Near the fires, you have to keep the pot holders visible: you don't have time to look for them when you need them. You can hang them or, if you don't like them in sight, keep them in a terracotta pot in which you can also put the wooden spoons.

40) Order the kitchen as if it were an archive.

41) If you have a chest of drawers with many small drawers, dedicate each one to a type of content: wooden or plastic spoons, caps, clips, chopper accessories, paper napkins, etc., and write the content on a label.

42) If you have different eating habits at home, write the names of each family member on the plastic containers in which you store the food in the refrigerator.

43) If every dry food (rice, pasta, grains, dried fruit, etc.) has a transparent container, you will always know what you have at home and when you have to buy back: avoid waste and unnecessary purchases.

44) Transfer the pasta and rice into transparent jars: the time it takes to do it when you come back from shopping, you regain it every time you cook, or you don't have to rummage through the packages.

45) Cut out pasta and rice cooking time and place it in the jars.

46) Keeping pasta and rice in jars allows you to have everything in view, avoiding forgetting leftovers at the bottom of the pantry.

47) Keeping pasta and rice in jars helps keep butterflies away.

48) Keeping pasta and rice in jars makes it easier for you when you have to fill out your shopping list because you can immediately see what you are missing and what is about to end.

49) Choose jars that are identical to each other, making it easier to stack or group them.

50) If you use dried fruit and seeds to put on salads or yogurt, group them in glass jars. Seeing what they contain and at what point they are consumed will help you keep your stock up to date.

51) If you use different types of flours (durum wheat, soft wheat 0 or 00, wholemeal, yellow, etc.), put them in glass jars and attach a label on each one.

52) Organize foods according to the expiry date: in front of those that expire first, behind the others.

53) To multiply the space. Split it!

54) Try to divide the interior spaces: a 60 cm or 90 cm wide basket is much better exploited if inside it fractions with smaller baskets.

55) In the 60 cm deep bases, insert baskets or pull-out metal or wood shelves to take out the contents and see them easily.

56) In a 60 cm deep base, there are 3 or 4 removable baskets 15 to 20 cm high. Allocate each to a type of object (salad bowls and serving bowls; containers for the refrigerator; canned foods; grains and flours; sweets and ingredients for cakes; everything needed for breakfast).

57) Insert shelves in the 60 cm deep wall units to divide the contents at different heights and depths. Find some ideas in the gallery!

58) To group trays, serving plates, and pans, you can insert a horizontal iron or metal bar 10/20 cm away from the bottom inside a wall unit: behind the bar, you will sort vertically, from the largest to the smallest, trays and serving dishes. Thus they will take up less space, and it will be easier to extract them.

59) An alternative for trays and plates: divide the space of the wall units with vertical wooden dividers, creating tall and narrow compartments in which to stow flat and large objects.

60) Allocate the deeper storage compartments to small appliances and the shallower ones to the food pantry.

61) For the pantry, shallow cabinets are enough: in 20/25 cm depth, you can comfortably 'store' all the food.

62) Tea towels take up less space if you keep them in a drawer rolled up in small cylinders.

63) A dead corner between the refrigerator and the wall can accommodate brooms or a small folding ladder: you can close it with a custom-made door if it is at least 20 cm wide.

64) If you love to keep things exposed, use the walls: on a bar with hooks, you can keep ladles, cutting boards, and small pans.

65) If you love to keep things exposed, you can hang cutting boards and other utensils on the walls even with simple nails, making them a decorative motif.

66) If you like things on display, use a pegboard to equip with small shelves and hooks to hang utensils.

67) If you are afraid that keeping a lot of things on display will give the kitchen a messy look, try to focus on colors: if, for example, you paint the wall a dark color and hang a metal bar, everything you hang will not stand out. But it will create a refined décor effect.

68) If you want everything to be indoors, take advantage of the internal side of the doors: you can hang the ladles, the special lids holders, and micro shelves for condiments, sugar, and honey.

69) The compartment under the sink is best used if you equip it with a removable rubbish basket.

70) In the compartment under the sink, use the upper part by hanging baskets for sponges and soap holders for dishes.

71) A shelf in the compartment under the sink can hold the rolls of garbage bags: just hang it 5/8 cm from the top of the compartment.

72) On the inside of the door under the sink, hang hooks to attach the sponges and well-wrung microfiber cloths.

73) With hooks hanging underneath an exposed shelf or in a cabinet, you can create an ad hoc space for hanging mugs and cups.

74) Group, do not pile.

75) Make sure that the contents of the drawers are all visible at the same time as soon as you open them.

76) Always use dividers in cutlery drawers.

78) If you have long items, divide the drawers with diagonal dividers to have longer compartments.

79) Do not choose too detailed cutlery dividers. Otherwise, you risk not being able to use them.

80) Separate cans and food in jars or bottles from that in cardboard boxes or bags.

81) If you have a pantry divided into several cabinets, set aside one for salty foods and one for sweets.

82) If you have utensils for special preparations, put them together in a box: for example, the tools for cake design or the necessary to prepare desserts (pastry bags, cookie cutters, molds for chocolates, birthday candles, etc.)

83) Create functional corners. For example, if you have a coffee machine, equip a compartment with everything you need for breakfast (rusks, jams, biscuits, sugar, cups, etc.) as close as possible.

84) Keep the plastic bags folded in small triangles inside a cardboard cylinder of the poster holders.

85) Collect bag-closing clips, rubber bands, and pliers in small boxes to put in a drawer.

86) If the kitchen storage compartments aren't enough, equip a trolley. The ideal is to dedicate it to a particular function: it brings condiments, spices, aromatic herbs, or everything you need for breakfast, or even for tea and snacks or liqueurs.

87) Not all cooking things go to the kitchen.

88) The small appliances that you use once in a while (e.g., ice cream maker, pasta machine, Versilia type ovens, ice crusher, etc.) can be placed in a closet or the upper part of the wall units.

89) The tablecloths that you do not use every day can be stored in a room other than the kitchen, for example, in a chest of drawers where you also store the sheets

90) Beautiful glasses, wine glasses, or sparkling wine glasses that you only use occasionally can fit in a piece of furniture in the living room.

91) The opposite rule also applies: in the kitchen, it is useful to keep things 'not from the kitchen': for example, a broom, a brush, and a dustpan. If they are small, the ideal space is under the sink; the long broom can hang on the wall: if you choose it beautiful, it will also be decorative.

92) Make your kitchen more functional with do-it-yourself tricks.

93) To keep the detergents with the sprayer tidy and visible, fix a horizontal bar in the door under the sink (such as those for clothes) and hang the sprayers for the 'spout.'

94) A document container applied to the inside of a door is perfect for holding parchment paper, film, and foil rolls.

95) On the inside of a door, the telephone number for assistance with faults for household appliances and a trusted plumber applies.

96) Leave inside the pantry or hang a notepad and a pencil from a door to write down what you are missing.

Making the shopping list a little at a time is more comfortable

97) Leave a glass container or cake pan with a transparent cloche full of dried fruit in sight and within reach: it's a healthy snack, and it's nice to see.

98) FINALLY ... Leave at least one drawer or a 'free' box to collect heterogeneous objects that do not fit into any group: there is no truly tidy room without its little 'mess corner'!

THE BUDGET

———— ◆◇◆ ————

M any factors determine the price of furniture because many variables come into play. It is impossible to give a single answer to the question, "how much does it cost to furnish a house." Still, we can provide you with interesting ideas and give you previews of projects that have already been completed so that you can understand what price range you might fall into.

The first piece of advice we give you is to list what you don't want to give up. We call it a wish list. From this, you can start defining an expense budget. With these two elements, our furniture consultants will advise you on products, solutions, materials, and appropriate accessories to create the furniture you have always dreamed of.

Our formula for calculating the cost of furniture

We thought of representing the cost of furniture with a formula, which obviously has no scientific claim, but which will surely make you think:

$$€ = (Q + d + \sqrt{P} + S) / fB$$

Q = Quality: design, materials, workmanship, durability, and attention to detail.

d = Dimensions: it is simple and perhaps a bit obvious, but a larger space needs more furniture.

P = Professionalism: many customers underestimate this aspect. A product without an adequate project is like a tree without leaves. We put it under the ground because it affects the price much less than expected.

S = Service: before, during, and after. We guarantee it.

fB = Bergamin factor: since we are leaders in our market segment, we can guarantee a price in line with the actual quality. Furthermore, our strength is the transversal nature of the offer and the alternatives we propose to you.

We have created three price ranges corresponding to different furnishing combinations using this formula. Since quality, service, and professionalism are always present, we have called them Premium, Gold, and Platinum.

Premium

Furnish your home with less than 10,000$. The kitchen certainly affects the cost of furniture. However, you can save a lot without regrets by choosing a linear and compact kitchen and accessing it with quality appliances without overdoing it (let's leave home automation for a moment). A likely price for a Premium kitchen is around $ 4,500.

Even for the living room and the sofa, many solutions can furnish with class and comfort with suitable materials and simple lines. $ 2,500, and the living area is ready.

We have to budget for a bed, a spacious wardrobe, a chest of drawers, and bedside tables in the sleeping area.

However, with not too difficult measures (both small and large), we can have a nice equipped room for 2,500 dollars.

Obviously, it does not end there: accessories, some rugs, a reading chair, and the very important lights and lamps. Five hundred dollars must be dedicated. There are tons of small budget solutions, such as furniture bonuses and renovation deductions, leading to big savings. Also, remember that we offer you the possibility to pay in installments at 0 interest and that in our stores, there is the Piazza Affari section, with super discounted furniture on display, which can be purchased

Also online!

Look at the personalized path we have dedicated to those who want to save.

Gold

Furnish your home for between $15,000 and $20,000. If your budget is a bit higher, you can afford a kitchen with a peninsula, a more advanced appliance kit, and play with different and more resistant materials. The cost goes up, hovering around $ 6,000.

We can add design pieces in the living room and introduce precious woods, such as knotted oak. Then, for moments of relaxation, we can indulge ourselves: sofas with peninsula or removable seats, armchairs, and poufs. For our Gold living area, we plan $ 4,000.

The bedroom is enriched with a particular furniture, such as a wardrobe in materic eco-wood or an upholstered bed. Depending on your wishes, we can range from just over $ 3,000 up to $ 4,500.

For accessories, it is more difficult to give a cost range, but certainly, with almost 2,000 dollars, you will be able to give the right personality to your home.

With this budget, it is very easy to build a beautiful house for a large family, which pays a lot of attention to everyone's space and needs. First, however, look at what we have studied for those who prefer practicality.

Platinum

Furnish your home with important budgets. If your priority is not attention to the wallet but having prestigious furniture that lasts forever and is technologically advanced, obviously, the solutions are endless. With all the brands and styles you can find in our stores, you will be spoiled for choice.

Kitchens with double depth, exclusive finishes, and appliances from the best brands on the market. Modular sofas with reclining backrests or removable seats. Design wall units and chairs. Luxury beds and mattresses with sliding wardrobes or hinged doors in precious materials. Greenlight to the most various furnishing accessories because we want to give life to a unique and precious home. Find out more about how we put competence and experience at the service of those looking for elegance and design.

The perfect kitchen - We define the budget

The kitchen is usually the most intimate and welcoming environment in your home. To enjoy it to the fullest, it is important not to leave anything to chance; only in this way will you create the right kitchen for you.

Establish your budget

First step: when planning a new kitchen, you need to establish the budget. **I know you were expecting a**

different or technical first point, but, in reality, it's the first thing to think about. The price range inherent in kitchens is enormous.

They range from "kitchens" of $ 890.00 (of which I do not know exactly the magic formula) to kitchens that far exceed the cost of your garage and sometimes of your apartment.

In large-scale distribution, sometimes, there are offers in which the kitchens have really low prices, but, in reality, they are the classic "decoy."

If one day you decide to buy one of these offers, know that for sure you will have to add transport and assembly costs that will affect from 10 to 20%, above all, you will have to take it exactly as reported in the advertisement because, as soon as you try a minimum of customization, the prices will skyrocket, reaching or even exceeding the price offered by your trusted decorator.

As for the "big names" who sell kitchens at very high prices, there is a bit of added value there. However, know that everything that certain names offer, such as particular finishes or materials, can also be found by purchasing kitchens from more commercial and perhaps even less well-known companies.

Obviously, even in this case, you will notice increases in the estimate, but they will certainly be more affordable sums. However, no matter how large the sum is at your disposal, even more, important will be how you intend to use it.

It will be important to focus on simplicity and, above all, decide from the start which part of the sum to allocate to furniture, household appliances, and accessories. You must consider your financial resources and your real needs to draw up a reliable list of the maximum budget for each item (kitchen furniture, appliances, etc.).

Keeping an eye on the budget is not a negative element; quite the contrary, it means emphasizing priorities and avoiding waste.

For example, being a lover of homemade products and dishes means needing a nice worktop made of water-repellent materials. So you can get your hands dirty and not that the doors have a visible or retractable handle. Finally, you need to keep priorities in mind. The trick to studying and defining your budget? Divide it according to the order of importance!

If you identify the focal point of your project, you will understand which elements to investing the most money in and which ones to consider in the background. Any other examples? Do you have little time for lunch or dinner?

You'll have even less to clean appliances. Therefore, invest in an induction hob, which can be cleaned with a rag, or in an oven with a self-cleaning function. If you like accessories and already have many to bring into the new kitchen, focus on useful and practical storage solutions and, why not, also creative.

On the other hand, if the most important thing for you is design and you are not interested in having the latest appliances, choose to spend more to have a really beautiful and trendy kitchen. Now that you have in mind your priorities, another piece of advice, always related to the budget, is not to fill all the spaces!

It may happen that, by defining the project, a number of square meters remain free in the room. In this case, do not simply add furniture to fill the shelves, wall units, or bookcases, which perhaps do not correspond to the real quantities of accessories to be housed.

How to do it? Start with an estimate of the objects you have (pots, plates, glasses, etc.), and consequently, you will understand how much actual storage space you will need so that each one finds its position.

Obviously, over time, the family could grow or shrink, and with it, your accessories; in the first case, remember that it is always possible to purchase additional container modules.

Finally, creativity! "Yes, ok, but how much does a kitchen cost ???" For example, today, a medium-level kitchen with class A appliances can be found at a price ranging from 3000 to 5000 dollars with a development of about 3.60mt. Obviously, this cost does not include table and chairs, while transport and assembly costs are at the discretion of the furniture maker.

Also, add your personal touch: screen printed backs, planters made from fruit crates, clocks made using old pallets, or whatever you can think of. By doing so, I am sure you will be able to create a unique and/or welcoming kitchen with the right investment.

HOW TO CHOOSE THE RIGHT LIGHTING FOR YOUR KITCHEN

———— ◆ ◇ ◆ ————

Lighting is often overlooked when designing a kitchen, but it is one of the most important elements for successful interior design. No matter how high-quality the materials are, how harmonious the color scheme is or how creative and well-executed your theme is, unsatisfactory lighting will leave a "dull" kitchen feeling.

Bright and cold overhead lighting makes your kitchen feel clinical and unwelcoming. Poor placement will leave dark spots in some places and cause light to "collect" in others, creating an uneven feel. Incorporating nothing but soft, low-level light could create a relaxing atmosphere, but it will be more difficult to cook and clean!

On the other hand, smart lighting brings out the best in any kitchen, enhancing favorite features and purposeful design choices while minimizing frustrations and diverting attention from any unpolished elements. A well-lit kitchen is a kitchen you'll enjoy spending time in, whether you're preparing a meal, entertaining guests, or just relaxing.

Before making any choice, it is important to understand how lighting inside a home works. No matter what the room is, there are three basic types of home lighting.

1. Ambient lighting

Also known as general lighting, ambient lighting is designed to create diffused and uniform light throughout a room; it is the type of light most associated with turning on a light switch. Ambient lighting is versatile and can take many forms, from ceiling lamps, chandeliers, and recessed ceiling lights to wall lights, valance lighting, track lighting, etc.

You can think of ambient light as the foundation for your general lighting scheme. Admittedly, it's not the most exciting element, but it's essential to get it right if you want to get amazing results.

2. Lighting of activities

Activity lighting is just what it sounds like - practical, focused, bright lights designed to help you do what you need to do. For example, it is used to illuminate worktops and other room areas for intensive use in a kitchen. Note that practically doesn't have to mean boring streaks of bright light, and well-lit areas provide a fantastic contrast to the softer parts of the kitchen and create nice tone variations. This atmospheric kitchen retains functionality and breaks up darker shades with bright LED strip lights on the sink and countertops.

There are both fixed and adjustable forms of activity lighting. Counter spotlights and pendant lights on a sink or dining table are the most common and illuminate the areas that need them most. Directional track lighting is also diffuse, where individual lights on a ceiling fitting can be adjusted to suit the room's needs.

3. Accent lighting

Accent lighting is the most creative but hardest form of lighting to achieve; remember that less often means more! The term immediately brings to mind the lighting that sets the mood and generates the mood of a room, but there are many other ways to highlight it.

Good accent lighting will draw attention to a particular artwork, décor, and design choices in your kitchen while diverting attention from elements that detract from the room's overall aesthetic.

Adjustable or dimmable lights allow you to change your kitchen's tone instantly. You can also use lighting to create interesting visual effects and signature pieces all by yourself.

This beautifully lit modern kitchen uses downward-pointing lights on the wall cabinets to illuminate the contents and create a striking patterned effect when closed.

These are not rigid categories: for example, a chandelier can provide ambient light on a dining table and function as accent lighting to set the room's mood, especially with a light intensity regulator. Likewise, adjustable lighting can light up a countertop in one minute and a favorite vase in the next.

Don't get too involved in technical terms. Instead, consider how the room is used, what you'd like to draw attention to, what you'd like to divert attention from and what you want your kitchen to look like. Achieve these goals, and you will naturally incorporate all the lighting you need.

I want to light like that of professionals: what should I consider? The bigger, the better. Recessed ceiling spotlights have become the preferred lighting for new kitchens, and a good reason: they are practical, customizable, and reliable.

However, they don't add much personality to a room! No matter the theme of your kitchen, a bold central light fitting can add a stunning finishing touch to your aesthetic. Chandeliers and sturdy pendant lights are experiencing a major resurgence in popularity, so there's never been a better time to put lighting in the center of your kitchen than as an afterthought.

These eye-catching candle effect chandeliers require attention and tie this charming rustic kitchen together.

Lights on the worktops. Under-cabinet lights are often the cheapest and easiest to install of all the changes you can make to your kitchen lighting. Battery-powered lights that attach to the underside of wall cabinets are inexpensive and instantly help illuminate the living space for prep.

You can purchase LED strip lights or duct tape to create a perfectly uniform lighting area. If you squint while preparing meals or prefer one well-lit section of the worktop over another, the lighting under the wall units will make a big difference.

Turn it on. Light intensity regulators and dimmable lamps are a wonderful addition to any kitchen. The ability to quickly choose how much light enters the room is underestimated: after installation, you will wonder how you ever lived without it. For technophiles, "smart lamps" can also be controlled via an app on your phone.

As it is above, so it is below. Lighting isn't just for the ceiling: the "plinth" lights under the base cabinets add an absorbing visual layer to your kitchen. If you're feeling purposeful, experiment with color variations to dramatically change the feel of the room in low light.

And these lights aren't just eye-catching; they're practical too, no more stumbling or bumping into the dark when looking for a midnight snack. In addition, the lighting under the central island in this bold and confident kitchen provides another element of visual interest.

69

HOW TO LIGHT UP THE KITCHEN? (3 MAIN POINTS TO CONSIDER)

———— ◆◇◆ ————

The lights in this room must satisfy two different and not necessarily complementary needs. On the one hand, kitchen lighting must be intense and energetic, which is functional for food preparation. But, on the other hand, it must also be warm and non-aggressive to encourage conviviality. **The question, therefore, arises spontaneously: how to illuminate the kitchen? Here are the three main points to consider!**

Kitchen lighting: what are the points where to install the light?

As is the case for all rooms, optimal lighting is obtained by combining background light (the base one), indirect light (peripheral), and functional light (targeted at the points where it is needed).

From this, it can already be deduced that the best solution would be to use more light points in the kitchen:

- A kitchen pendant light on the table (background / functional lighting),
- Spotlights above the wall units (for a scenographic effect)
- Kitchen wall lamps or led strips (as indirect lighting),
- Other suspensions for the kitchen or led strips (complement functional lighting).

Dining table

One of the main areas is the table: the point on which a pendant lamp should be lowered. Kitchen chandeliers, if used exclusively for the table, should have lights directed downwards and be installed at the optimal height to illuminate the entire surface best. In this case, the suspension would be used as a functional light. However, since the table is usually located in the center of the room, the chandeliers for the kitchen are also used as the main light source (therefore for background lighting).

This dual function it fulfills makes the chandelier should be considered the main element from which to start planning the lighting in the kitchen. In this regard, you may also be interested in "How to light up the table in the kitchen or the dining room."

Kitchen wall lamp for indirect lighting

Once you have chosen the main light source, you need to focus on the peripheral areas of the kitchen. This avoids creating shaded areas that make the room seem darker and less livable. You can choose wall lights or even LED strips with a beam of light aimed mainly upwards for the less illuminated corners.

Functional lighting for worktops

How to perfectly illuminate a kitchen without considering the various work surfaces? Impossible! When cooking, it is customary to use various flat surfaces to cut, knead, blend, etc. To carry out all these actions, you need adequate light: intense, white, and directed exactly where you are working.

But if the table is already well served by the chandelier, the same thing does not necessarily apply to the kitchen cabinet tops, which are usually located at the ends of the room and in a dimly lit area. In this case, a dedicated light would be needed! For example, we can install LED strips under the cabinets of the cabinet so that the entire area below is properly illuminated.

For work surfaces such as islands and peninsulas, on the other hand, it is always possible to choose suspensions but soberer than the one positioned on the table (in order not to diminish their aesthetic value). Given the lack of space on the top of the island or peninsula, one or more pendant lamps are ideal for obtaining a direct beam of light from the relative floors.

Kitchen ceiling lights

In some cases, however, the best solution might be to focus on a single light source that fulfills all three needs (background light, indirect and functional). For example, if you have a rather small kitchen with low ceilings or if you cannot modify/integrate the electrical system, a ceiling lamp would be the obvious choice!

The kitchen ceiling light can be installed above the table and as background light to illuminate the whole room better. The kitchen ceiling lights, like the suspensions, are available in different styles, colors, sizes, and models, so you will certainly have the possibility to find the one you like best, and that can fully reflect the style of the whole room.

Beautify The Kitchen In All Seasons

Here are ten quick ways to embellish and change the face of the kitchen environment without spending a fortune. Renovating the kitchen with low-cost ideas is an alternative way to proceed with renovation without spending a fortune. In this way, the functionality remains intact while using tricks, objects, and decorations as a form of embellishment most suitable to bring back to life and renew that furniture that seems aged and not very current.

Ten ideas:

- Paint the doors
- Furniture cover curtains
- Change the door handles
- Faux tiles
- Change the floor
- Faucet
- Splash guard panel
- Rustic table
- Shelves
- Decorate with dishes

Beautifying old kitchen: inspirations

The possibility of saving some money to devote to other activities and expenses, such as a vacation, the purchase of a car, or an urgent medical expense, could be the first cause of obstacle to the renovation of a room of the house that is very exploited and used as the kitchen.

Hence it is urgent to resort to the imagination to avoid letting the wall units fall to pieces, seeing the doors yellowed, or having a refrigerator that seems to have been recovered from an antique shop, although it is still functional.

Ten low-cost decorations for Christmas day: tips and ideas

If the doors have a faded white, they can be repainted with pastel colors or fluorescent colors when you want to have an environment with futuristic tones.

Instead, replacing the hob can be an affordable expense, perhaps opting for an induction hob that will avoid the use of gas and will require a simple power outlet. A series of new appliances with a particular design and high performance will be the way to renew the worktop, saving time in preparing dishes and having safer tools and numerous options available.

Ten low-cost ideas to embellish the old kitchen

We have just moved to a new city for work and study purposes, and already paying the rent can be an expense that affects your budget a lot. Or the elderly aunt gave us an apartment in the countryside where we can go for weekends or summer holidays.

Renovating the kitchen

And we realize that the furniture seems a little backward for our tastes. However, the arrangement of the furniture and wall units is still functional, suitable for our purposes, and where you can still work comfortably.

Paint the doors

If you have a wooden kitchen, the best way to change its face is to paint the doors of the cabinets and furniture. Then, depending on your preferences and taste, you can think about giving a nice refresh, opting for pastel colors if you want a soft environment, or experimenting with contrasting combinations if you feel more bohemian and ethnic.

Furniture cover curtains

Surely you will be very fond of your grandmother's furniture, which presents a story that goes back a long way and which you are fond of because they remind you of your childhood. Unfortunately, however, the years may have scratched their beauty, with slight yellowing or breakage signs that make them ugly.

A series of curtains can avoid showing you the doors marked by time and for which you are undecided on which colors to adopt. Replacing them with a nice curtain, perhaps made by a tailor or with your own hands, immediately changes the room's appearance.

Change the door handles

A quick and painless pit stop: are the old door handles rusted and have lost their enamel? You can think of replacing them with modern and colorful models, always functional, giving luster to the drawers. The only necessary precaution will be to be careful to seal the holes of the previous handles so as not to leave traces of the past.

Fake tiles

The old tiles have tired you, but you have no intention of changing them. Don't worry: you can use self-adhesive papers whose range of colors, geometric textures, and patterns will leave you speechless. In addition, the adhesive papers are produced in such a way as to obtain the effect of natural materials such as stone, wood, or ceramic.

These are products made so well that they look natural, and then when cleaning, a damp cloth will be enough to remove any residue of dirt. Then, detach them to choose another texture when you want to change.

Change the floor

The floor is one of the first things to pay attention to when entering a room. Observing an old surface, which seems outdated, always makes the environment gloomy.

Laminate can be the right solution that makes the room more modern: it can be placed on top of the previous surface, thus avoiding more expensive masonry work and thus avoiding the formation of dust and debris.

The proposals are almost endless on the market, both for textures and colors and for the similarity with natural materials such as stone and wood. Cleaning will also be easier, taking just a few minutes a day.

Faucet

A low-cost intervention in every sense and with a low impact is to change the mixer of the kitchen sink. A breath of fresh air is possible, reducing the final cost to tens of euros. Taking a tour of the DIY and DIY stores, you can find truly innovative models that will give a more elegant and chic touch.

Splash guard panel

Preserve the wall from splashes of food and fat while preparing the dishes and, at the same time, have a colorful and lively cooking area: replacing the splash guard panel is an uncomplicated operation that requires some time and a few tools at hand.

Resin and glass are the most suitable materials for the change and renovation of the room, being able to choose on the market a variety of models that differ in colors and patterns and some interesting proposals for views of cities of art, mountains or sea. You can also choose to have LED lighting that makes the proposal futuristic or adopt a steel panel if your priority is resistance to high temperatures.

Rustic table

Do you have a backward kitchen from all points of view? Change the table and match it to the environment: a rustic proposal with country tones will be adequate. Or, if you like to pickle the furniture, make it in a shabby chic or Provencal style: the country air will always inspire you.

Shelves

The shelves can solve the age-old problem of lack of space in the room, become an open-air wardrobe without doors, and become a support surface to embellish by putting some plants, souvenir photos, or cheerful transparent glass jars for the most consumed products. In this way, you have more space, have many valuable things in sight, and can renovate in a low-cost way.

Decorate with plates

Simple and typical of restaurants and taverns, arranging colored plates on the walls in a confused way, letting oneself go to the imagination, becomes an alternative world to paint, more expensive and requires greater effort. We recommend reading the article: Beautifying walls with dishes for further suggestions on the subject.

Materials for the kitchen top

The choice of the kitchen top is fundamental in the design of the kitchen because it is the stylistic completion. Particularly in modern homes, where the kitchen and living room interact directly, the top is the center of attention, often the protagonist of islands and peninsulas. Its style gives design and character to the whole environment, and to be sure to choose the best materials for the kitchen tops; there are many variables to consider.

Reaching the right balance between aesthetics and functionality may not seem simple; aesthetics are important as an exposed kitchen component. To best complete the furniture, the top must be beautiful and maintain its appearance for a long time, even if subjected to various culinary activities.

In a highly technical environment such as the kitchen, the worktop will be subjected to the action of water, detergents, and acids, and hot pots, heavy objects, and sharp objects will likely be placed on it. All harmless actions, which also risk irreparably damaging this component, and knowing the best materials for kitchen tops, will allow you to offer your customers a quality and long-lasting product.

What a quality kitchen top must be like

The top must be practical, easy to clean, keep clean, and give freedom of action and movement to those who live in the kitchen every day. Cutting food without a special cutting board, simply placing a hot pot, without using a trivet for protection, contact with water or aggressive chemical agents, or splashes of acidic elements such as lemon, tomato, or vinegar, are included in those daily activities that can damage the beauty of a worktop.

The choice of material should therefore not be underestimated; the customer should be informed about the best materials for kitchen tops available on the market to allow him to make a choice suited to his needs and his spending possibilities.

Often customers who are preparing to buy a kitchen are confused by the many options available on the market and turn to retailers and designers to understand which are the best materials for kitchen tops.

The proposals on the market are innumerable, it is possible to choose between many colors, effects, and finishes, but it is the material of which the worktop is made that makes the difference.

It is difficult to understand in advance whether to prefer an economical but practical worktop or a beautiful top that requires care and maintenance. Customers should be informed about the properties and advantages of the various materials and then, according to their needs, guided in the best choice. **Remember that the kitchen top is not a detail but the protagonist of the kitchen.**

Manufacturers are always looking for the most technological and innovative materials to guarantee the quality, durability, and aesthetic performance at the highest possible levels. On the market, some tops are made with the best materials that can guarantee quality, durability, and practicality even in the face of intensive and sometimes unscrupulous use. A poor quality material could save you money at first, but over time it could lead to problems such as discoloration or the appearance of indelible stains, and even swelling near the joints.

What are the best materials for kitchen tops

There is no perfect material for all customers. Everyone has their own needs and aesthetic preferences, so some prefer natural stones while others choose laminate.

Each material has properties and advantages, but only some can guarantee incorruptibility and aesthetic stability over time, even in the face of the most intensive activities. So let's see together what are the best materials available to make kitchen tops.

1. Laminate

It is a versatile material aesthetically, replicating even the most precious materials aesthetically. Among the advantage of laminate is undoubtedly the price. In fact, it is an inexpensive material, really convenient compared to other tops, and it is also very resistant to scratches and bumps.

It is stain resistant, easy to clean, and requires very little maintenance. It is possible to make it in many colors, and it finishes to adapt to the style of the kitchen; however, it is very sensitive to heat and discoloration due to the sun's rays. It is also susceptible to infiltration of water and steam near the joints. For this reason, despite its undeniable qualities, it is not possible to include it among the best materials for kitchen tops.

2. HPL laminate

The search for new functional solutions for the kitchen has given rise to innovative materials, such as layered HPL (high pressure) laminate, an evolution of the more common laminate, capable of satisfying the increasingly demanding requests for style and functionality.

It is a laminate composed of layers of cellulose fibers combined with thermosetting resins, which, subject to a simultaneous application of pressure and heat, give life to a non-porous, homogeneous material that can be given the surface finish requested by the customer.

This technological process makes it a resistant material, both to water and heat, something that the standard laminate cannot ensure. It is also pleasant to the touch, thanks to its silkiness.

3. Natural stones: marble and granite

For those who love the expressive power of natural stones and want to give an elegant and material touch to their kitchen, granite and marble are among the best materials for kitchen tops.

The granite

It is a durable and resistant material, which has always been synonymous with strength and is capable of giving character to the kitchens in which it is inserted. It is a natural stone; therefore, it shows a certain porosity, but it can resist acids better than marble; it has a greater ability to resist shocks and maintain its appearance unchanged over time.

The marble

It is the material chosen by those who want to create a fine kitchen that can resist the fashions of the moment. With its typical and unrepeatable veins, marble can embellish any space and gives the kitchen a timeless elegance, more than any other material. It is available in many colors and finishes to adapt to every taste and style requirement.

Always used in luxury kitchens, it also guarantees a highly hygienic surface, where you can cook with peace of mind but always with some attention. However, marble is more delicate than granite, a too violent impact could cause the marble slab to break, and chemical agents or acid substances can stain it. A protective product is applied in quality kitchens to make it waterproof, but its porous nature still puts it at risk of infiltration.

It always remains one of the best materials for kitchen tops, both in classic and modern style, precisely because of its timeless style, and with due attention, it is possible to make the marble top last for many years.

4. Quartz

Quartz is one of the most precious minerals found in nature and one of the best materials for kitchen tops. For the tops, we talk about quartz agglomerates. They are materials made up of about 95% natural quartz with the addition of components such as glass, colored pigments, or resins to improve their aesthetic performance and durability. The result is a top with brilliant and unique textures, a smooth and non-porous top, therefore impermeable to liquids, highly hygienic, and antibacterial.

It is a performing material capable of lasting over time because it is very resistant to daily stresses, stains, acids, and abrasions; it is also easy to maintain and does not require excessive care. However, attention should be paid to boiling pots because quartz is not extremely heat resistant: placing a pot that has just been removed from the heat on the hob without the necessary precautions could irretrievably mark it or even break it.

It is a material widely used in modern kitchen compositions. The wide choice of colors and finishes allows you to create designer kitchens with great aesthetic value and are functional and durable at the same time. In addition, it allows great customization and the creation of integrated sinks, even if the under-top sink solution is preferred.

5. Steel

The hygienic properties of this material make it particularly suitable for use in the kitchen, which is why it is considered among the best materials for kitchen tops. It has an almost infinite life, excellent impact resistance, and is very easy to clean, some types of steel are prone to scratches and limescale stains, but with a bit of attention and unique products, the steel will be as bright and shiny as the first day. It is widely used in modern kitchens for the minimal look it gives to the kitchen and in professional kitchens for its hygienic and highly practical qualities. However, detractors consider steel to be cold and not very innovative.

6. Corian

Corian is made from ductile and easy-to-work resins, capable of creating joint-free products, which are unsightly in a modern environment and could be a breeding ground for germs and dirt. It is one of the best materials for kitchen tops, but it is also widely used in luxury bathrooms and for the creation of design furnishing accessories. It has a very long life and is resistant to the heaviest culinary activities.

Of great aesthetic beauty, Corian is often used to create peninsulas and islands in continuity with the kitchen top and sinks integrated into the top to give taste and design to modern kitchens. Its peculiarities include creating curved worktops, giving life to highly personalized and creative kitchens, and the possibility of restoring small abrasions or scratches directly on site, without disassembly.

It is a resistant material and represents a cutting-edge choice in kitchen furnishing; however, if your customers are oriented to the choice of Corian, suggest them to pay careful attention to high heat sources, such as pots just removed from the fire. Or irons.

7. Dekton

Dekton results from continuous research and innovation in the furniture sector; it is an agglomeration of natural materials such as glass, ceramic, and quartz. It is also ideal for intensive use of worktops because it can withstand scratches, bumps, abrasions, fire and heat, and chemical and acid stains. At the moment, it is not only among the best materials for kitchen tops but also guaranteed against thermal shock.

It is a product capable of offering a smooth, non-porous surface with a high aesthetic value, pleasant to the touch, and, with its large-format slabs available in different thicknesses, it is possible to cover large surfaces without joints. In addition, it is perfect for modern kitchens because it allows the creation of kitchens with a sink integrated into the top, ideal for those who love clean lines and the visual continuity of this stylistic solution. Available in many colors and finishes, some can replicate the veins of marble or oxidized metal.

8. Laminam

Laminam is a cutting-edge material capable of guaranteeing a worktop resistant to all types of mechanical stress but also incredibly beautiful to look at. It is a large-format ceramic slab, 1000x3000mm, available in multiple colors and achievable in different thicknesses and profiles to adapt to any context and furnishings. The advantages of a Laminam top are essentially the design, truly elegant and refined, combined with unparalleled quality characteristics:

- It is resistant to frost and heat.
- It is easy to clean, and hot water and neutral detergents are sufficient.s
- It does not fear aggressive agents such as limescale remover.

WAYS TO FURNISH AN ELECTRIC STYLE KITCHEN

———— ◆◇◆ ————

Furnishing a kitchen in an eclectic style: here are our tips for doing it better without making mistakes. The right colors, the most suitable finishes and materials, which palettes to use, and what is the right atmosphere to recreate in your eclectic style kitchen.

The word eclectic immediately makes us think of something variable, heterogeneous, and creative without a precise address. On the contrary, the eclectic one is a style that has no fixed rules but which plays with bizarre references, bold combinations, variable colors, and original palettes.

It is an extravagant style that focuses on innovation and, at times, can be eccentric or bold, therefore suitable for those who love courageous contrasts and want an environment that does not go unnoticed.

However, despite what one might believe, the eclectic style is not messy, and even if there are no precise rules for making them, there are principles to be respected to get the right atmosphere. In this article, we want to give you some tips for decorating an eclectic style kitchen.

Eclectic style

The kitchen can be considered a real laboratory, the forge of the house, where it is created, where dishes are prepared for oneself and for loved ones: the eclectic style is perfect to describe all the creative spirit that one breathes in the kitchen.

Contemporary interior design has already passionately adopted the eclectic style for the whole house, especially in the living area, which is particularly suitable for furnishing with this look. The idea of a beautiful eclectic style kitchen, on the other hand, is more recent because, for the kitchen, a simple, clean, minimal or classic, or shabby chic style is usually preferred. Yet, as you will see in the solutions we are about to show you, the eclectic style is particularly suitable for enhancing the creativity that must be breathed in any self-respecting kitchen.

At the bottom of the article, you will always find a rich gallery of images to inspire you and thus furnish your delicious kitchen in an eclectic style.

Blue and white for a marine atmosphere of yesteryear

1. Extravagant wall and floor coverings
2. Eclectic but minimalist cuisine
3. A new antique combination for an ultra-modern kitchen
4. Eclectic cuisine with industrial touches
5. The charm of vintage reinterpreted by the eclectic style

Furnishing a kitchen in an eclectic style: images and photos

Blue and white for a marine atmosphere of yesteryear. The first solution that we show you is an eclectic style kitchen that takes up the slightly vintage atmosphere of beach houses and transforms it into a modern and romantic look, thanks to the use of white with touches of navy blue. The decoration on the wall is beautiful, in full eclectic style, which takes up the color of the table feet.

All the rest of the kitchen is white, very bright, and with vintage lines of furniture and details. The result is a balanced mix of past and present that will certainly fascinate those who love maritime atmospheres.

Rules for decorating your home in an eclectic style

1. Extravagant wall and floor coverings

To obtain a very original kitchen that certainly will not go unnoticed, we advise you, if you have the possibility, to pay attention to the choice of coverings, both for the walls and for the floor. It is certainly a very delicate and fundamental choice, which we recommend only to those who are not afraid of getting bored and love contrasts.

The effect is certainly very original but also extravagant, so opt for this solution only if you are prepared for the idea of an atmosphere of constant and desired disorder. If you choose to decorate your kitchen with a mix of extravagant coverings, remember that the rest of the furniture should preferably be minimal and sober to avoid a chaotic result.

2. Eclectic but minimalist cuisine

The eclectic style does not necessarily have to be synonymous with orderly chaos and extravagance; you may also love the minimal style but want an eclectic atmosphere. The solution is what we show you below. As you can see, the kitchen is tidy and very simple, thanks to a very sober color palette that includes white, wood, steel, and black, thanks to straight lines and a study of very precise spaces.

For example, the eclectic atmosphere combines different materials, steel and wood, and heterogeneous styles, such as the wooden and black lacquered steel table, with an industrial flavor and the plastic chairs with sinuous lines from the 1960s.

3. A new antique combination for an ultra-modern kitchen

Old and new come together in this beautiful kitchen, which results from combining lines with a vintage flavor. The kitchen furniture, for example, has very modern elements and details, the lighting or the peninsula. The result is a mix of new and old that gives eclecticism to the environment.

4. Eclectic cuisine with industrial touches

If you love the industrial style, but like reinterpreting it with an eclectic look, the solution is obtained with furniture with a rough finish, neutral palette, and materials such as steel, wood, and stone. The touch of class is the lighting obtained with many pendant lamps that will give the right industrial and eclectic flavor to the environment.

5. The charm of vintage reinterpreted by the eclectic style

A kitchen with a vintage style but a modern and eclectic atmosphere is obtained by skilfully combining materials and colors. The cut of the furniture is vintage, but the lighting, for example, is industrial and the modern colors, especially the contrasting ones such as the beautiful mint green chairs.

KITCHEN SINK

———— ◆◇◆ ————

Before deciding what size and shape your kitchen sink will have, think about how you behave in this environment and your habits. You should understand which model will be more congenial to you, even evaluating customized or less common solutions. On the other hand, if you have a small kitchen, perhaps the spaces themselves will dictate its shape and size. Remember, however, that even the sink can contribute to furnishing and personalizing this environment, so it is a detail to be chosen with due attention. In this Ideabook, you will find some ideas to understand which could be the right sink for you.

The choice of the sink depends on the space available to you and your environment. There are no rules or standard measures; the kitchen is one of the most versatile rooms. Therefore, you can enjoy designing it, respecting your tastes and needs. Remember, though, that the location of the drains will determine the shape and, more importantly, the location of your sink.

The measurements of the single bowl sink range from 40 to 100 cm in width. Generally, if space permits, the most used model is the rectangular one with a drip tray that measures 100 cm in width and 55 cm in depth.

The shape of the sink is independent of the choice of materials and, in particular, of the type of built-in. To the classic solution, with the sink resting on the top protruding by a few millimeters, you can prefer flush, semi-top, or under-mount models. The latter guarantees more space and, therefore, more freedom of movement.

The small (40-45 cm), practical, and recessed single bowl sink is ideal if your kitchen is not very large. But it is also interesting if you have a large room and have decided to design a second sink on the central island. Remember, however, the need for dual exhausts.

If your kitchen is small and cramped and you choose the single-bowl sink due to space constraints, it is usually good to place it at the end of the counter. If, on the other hand, you have opted for this solution to have a second countertop sink, it may be more practical to place it in the center of the island.

With two tanks

The double basin is more practical if you love to cook, have a large family, or often have guests for dinner. The sink with two identical bowls without a side drainer measures approximately 80 centimeters. If you do not want to take away any additional space from your worktop, you can choose a type with a rear drip, longer and shallower than the solution on the side of the tubs.

A convenient idea if you already have a dish drainer in the cabinets above the sink. However, I prefer the classic drip tray next to the tubs if you don't have a dishwasher or if you don't like to use it frequently. Remember that the two bowl sink with a side drainer measures approximately 120 centimeters.

At sight

You may prefer a sink built into the top that remains visible in the front to the more classic types. It can be flush, or, if you prefer, it can even protrude a few millimeters from the kitchen cabinets. Again, a typically custom-designed solution that helps personalize your environment. Again, you can choose a sink with one or two bowls. The latter takes up more space.

To steel, a more practical and linear material, you can prefer ceramic, aesthetically more interesting in particular if colored, but with thicker profiles. This material is hygienic, easy to clean, and does not absorb odors but requires care and attention as it can chip off more easily.

In addition to steel and ceramics, you can opt for synthetic materials: much loved, they are composed of natural stones and resins and resist heat and even scratches and bumps.

With two separate tanks

If you choose a sink with two separate bowls, you are free to decide their size according to your needs. It takes up more space than the classic sink with two adjacent bowls, but it is aesthetically more impactful, ideal if you don't have space problems, and has a long linear top.

Remember that the compartment under the sink, already occupied by the drains, is generally used to place a removable drawer with the bins and, very often, a second drawer, just below the tubs, smaller and always removable, which can be useful for place small tools.

When the measures are different

The second tank is practical, even if small, especially if you love to cook. It becomes valid support if, for example, you want to leave the vegetables in water or quickly rinse the cutlery. But surely, if tight, it does not allow you to rinse large dishes or pots. A sink with two basins of different sizes without a drip tray measures approximately 60 centimeters.

If your kitchen has a particular size, you can replace the single bowl sink with an irregularly shaped two bowl sink. It allows you to replace the classic type, square or round, with a different model, which guarantees better space optimization.

Angled

The corner sink is not the simplest solution, yet sometimes necessary if the kitchen is small or uneven. Unfortunately, there are not many models on the market. Better to prefer the version with two in-line bowls and a 90 ° drip tray.

Accessories to integrate

Depending on the size of your tub, you can add matching accessories. For example, cutting boards or modules integrated above the sink become practical support surfaces for cooking. Likewise, you can add grids, trays for washing fruit and vegetables, or modules to be applied to the drain to retain food residues.

Here is an example of a single bowl sink placed on the top with a drainer. These solutions have different sizes, to be chosen according to the characteristics of your kitchen. However, a similar type sacrifices the top: it is, therefore, advisable if you have a large countertop in another part of the room.

HOME AUTOMATION KITCHEN: HOW TO MAKE WORK IN THE KITCHEN SMART

---◆◇◆---

What is meant by home automation? What devices can we install? How can you make kitchen management easier? Practical solutions to facilitate cooking activities. The evolution of home automation inside the apartments is made possible thanks to the brands' continuous research to make the living experience more and more comfortable.

It is no coincidence that the term has its origins in the Latin "Domus," which means home, and from telematics, it thus represents the discipline that allows you to automate the house, in which computer science and artificial intelligence come together almost to have many small robots ready to help us in the daily management.

But home automation also means safety, simplicity, and speed, and you will be amazed by the possibility of having general control of the whole kitchen with a simple touch. The communication network created throughout the room with which we can interact simultaneously is the true nature of home automation.

From household appliances to video surveillance, temperature and consumption control, switching on the heating system, lights, and the boiler are just some advantages of installing smart devices. Let's discover some items that cannot be missing in a kitchen marked by innovation.

- Smart lights and sockets
- Smart cooking top
- Management of household appliances
- Smart thermostat
- The Smart sink
- Voice Assistant
- Smart security

How to set up a home automation kitchen photos and images

- Smart lights and sockets: smart light bulbs and sockets have been very popular items in recent years; their success is mainly due to their ease of use and installation, but above all to the ability to remotely manage the electrical system via the smartphone or tablet.

  We would no longer worry about having left the kitchen lights on, and in the morning, when we wake up, we can turn on the socket of the coffee machine from the comfort of the bed.

- Smart hob: is a completely innovative and intuitive technology with smart commands and settings with remote management. For example, through a simple application on the mobile phone, it is possible to control the power of the plates on and control their switching off and manage electricity consumption. Some manufacturers have also introduced recipe books with which to help you during the preparation of the dishes, all handy solutions that emphasize the concept of comfort.

Ideas for designing a home automation kitchen

Management of household appliances

It is known that the kitchen and food play a central role in an apartment, and it is no coincidence that it is the most lived-in room. Therefore, most of the appliances in circulation are equipped with a wifi connection and wireless management for control via the application.

Smart refrigerators can be equipped with a monitor that allows you to view the food contained inside, thus avoiding continuous opening without the risk of causing thermal shock to the food itself. Through the application, you can control the set temperature and the internal view of the appliance, manage its consumption, and even warn of the expiry of a food.

An interesting feature of refrigerators equipped with a screen is that they can remotely send messages to the device that will remain a reminder on display and can be seen by those who have stayed at home or on our return.

Coffee machines, food processors, dishwashers, microwaves, and classic ovens are all kitchen appliances that have hailed the old way of working to become smart.

Smart thermostat

The heating system is usually installed throughout the apartment, even in the less-used rooms; this often forces us to open and close the water supply in some house rooms.

The installation of a smart thermostat that controls the operation of the boiler and, at the same time, of all the radiators is the right choice if you want to personally control the heating of the rooms without being forced to close them completely. As a result, it will no longer happen to have excessively hot rooms and other glacial ones.

The application can be used to set the preferred temperature allowing global warming of the entire apartment. To manage the radiators individually, there are special programmable thermostatic valves on the market; the application manages the timer. We will thus have the ability to manage everything individually, also containing consumption.

THE SMART SINK

———— ◆◇◆ ————

The cleanliness of food and the associated water consumption will no longer be a problem with the smart sink. One of the latest inventions in home automation is creating an ultrasonic cleaning system that reduces consumption and avoids food spoilage, guaranteeing the perfect cleanliness of the food.

Voice Assistant

The Voice Assistants can enhance smart management of the kitchen and the entire apartment. These are devices that, recognizing the voice and therefore also the command dictated, can execute it.

It is possible to connect them to wifi and configure them with our control device; the pairing to all smart items is intuitive and makes their management even faster. Moreover, it will not be necessary to enter every single application but ask the assistant what to do.

Smart security

A home automation kitchen does not only mean avant-garde and ease but, above all, safety, a feature increasingly sought after by consumers and every manufacturer dedicates great effort. As a result, every smart appliance we can install in the kitchen has a safety function that keeps us away from any inconvenience, from short circuits to water leaks.

They are also able to notify anomalies or malfunction of the device itself. It will also be possible to remedy in time because they allow timely connection with the dedicated service centers that will help us find the right solution for our needs or plan the intervention of a specialized technician.

How to set up a home automation kitchen photos and images

You can see some interesting home automation kitchen solutions and ideas in the gallery that can make your work even more fun and simple.

How to renovate the kitchen without completely changing it

Paint, wallpaper, laminate flooring All these tools, easy to use and inexpensive, are enough to renew your kitchen immediately. They are clean, quick solutions that you can make yourself in a few hours. Give it a try, and you will see how these simple decorative resources will completely transform the environment. When you are done, your kitchen will look like another.

1. Change the color of the furniture

If you are tired of your color, give it a coat of paint. It's the fastest and cheapest way to transform a kitchen out of style. If the furniture is white, even just changing the color of the lower ones will get you a nice makeover. If they are made of melamine, the most common material, use a lacquer affect enamel. First, however, sand the surfaces a little with sandpaper to make the paint adhere better and apply two or three coats (the first you need as a sealant), letting it dry between one and the other.

In addition to enamel, there are also specific products on the market for painting kitchen furniture: you will find them indicated in the package. The range of colors is very wide, and so are the finishes: matte, satin, bright, and extra bright. The result will surprise you.

2. Paint the tiles

One idea for renovating damaged kitchen tiles is to paint them. The work is not as boring as it may seem, and the walls have an amazing effect. You can find special paints for ceramic surfaces on the market, formulated to eliminate the need to apply other products, such as sealants or primers.

These glazes are easily applied with a roller, which withstands humidity very well and guarantees very durable and resistant finishes. Also, once the paint is dry, it can be washed off without risking peeling or blistering. High-quality paint brands have the right products for this type of application.

3. Choose fake tiles

There are self-adhesive wallpapers with rollers or large-format foils with prints that imitate natural materials, such as stone, wood, or tiles, which will allow you to achieve the effect we see in this kitchen. You can find a great variety of models, with the most eye-catching and disparate combinations.

These cards are so well made that they look almost real, and, in addition, they can be washed with a damp cloth to remove grease or grime residue. Next, they are applied directly to the surface, which must be cleaned well to adhere without problems. Then, when you get tired, you can easily detach them.

4. Apply decorative stickers

If you think that your kitchen has gone out of fashion or that it no longer communicates with you, but you are not ready for the complications of a real renovation, try renovating it with stickers. They are perfect for decorating kitchen doors or bringing out small details in one or more walls, as in the example in the photo.

After choosing the sticker with the motif you like best, you just have to remove the protective paper a little at a time and attach it to the wall. It is very important to make it smooth as you apply it to prevent bubbles or lines from forming.

5. Lay a laminate floor

Laminate is a nice solution for modernizing kitchen floors because, by placing it on top of the original, it prevents the formation of dust and debris during the work. There are an infinite number of decorative options, even with geometric shapes and imitations of natural materials such as stone and wood. With a vinyl finish, it can be washed without problems.

Since it is presented in planks, installation is very simple: each piece has a groove on one side and a tab to ensure that the pieces fit together without fixing materials. There is no need to glue or screw them to the existing floor.

It is only necessary to level the floor with a specific paste if there are any irregularities; otherwise, they can be placed on top of the old floor in no time. Depending on the laminate, it may be advisable to lay a special underlay mat. You will realize that it is enough to renovate the floor to modernize the entire kitchen. Another original proposal, if the kitchen tiles are divided into two areas, is to use two buts.

TOTAL KITCHEN COST: FROM DESIGN TO INSTALLATION

———— ◆◇◆ ————

How to design a kitchen? Prices according to what do they change? And what are the styles and compositions to choose from? Choosing to renovate the kitchen is certainly a choice that must be carefully considered. It requires an important economic investment and a piece of furniture that will last over the years. However, when the time comes to design a bespoke kitchen, whether to renovate an old one or because we have bought a new home, we don't always know where to start!

There are to consider the arrangement of the functional areas, from where to place the hob to where to place the refrigerator, but also to deal with the space actually available and decide on the style, composition, and finishes. To make this easier, it is best to ask for help from an industry professional.

Price table

Once you have received the quotes for the kitchen design and prices in hand, it will be easy to make the right choice. You will also be able to read reviews from past customers to make the situation even clearer. First of all, it's a good idea to check out our average kitchen design pricing table to get a comprehensive and realistic overview of the final cost.

Kitchen design prices	from	to
Consultancy cost	$ 200	$ 15,000
Economy range kitchen	$ 1000	$ 5000
Mid-range kitchen	$ 6,000	$ 10,000
Luxury range kitchen	$ 15,000	$ 25,000
Hourly labor cost	$ 25	$ 50

PLEASE NOTE that prices may vary due to the type of work, the quality of its execution, and your region.

Factors affecting the kitchen budget

When designing a kitchen, prices vary greatly depending on a few decisive factors. First of all, the linear meters of the kitchen count, therefore the dimensions, any unexpected events during the work, the type of composition, and the choice of masonry or modular model. Other factors affect the final cost of the kitchen;

Brand: it is a fundamental element because the kitchen design price mainly depends on it. There are well-known and advertised brands that require a much larger investment than other, more accessible brands.

Household appliances: In this case, we start from low-cost products to more and more technological and innovative ones. Hob, refrigerator, oven, and dishwasher are often excluded from the price of the composition precisely because they have a decisive influence on the final estimate.

Finishes: the materials are perhaps what should be chosen with the most care since they determine the kitchen's aesthetics and its entire sound; after a few years, you will notice the difference between mediocre material and valuable material.

Taps and fittings: the most modern and original models, perhaps even design ones, certainly have higher prices than the classic ones; in this case, you have to choose the ones that best suit the style of your kitchen.

How to design the kitchen: materials and prices

Designing a kitchen also means choosing the materials or the finishes that characterize the composition. Here are the materials most frequently used to make today's kitchens:

- Metal kitchens are perfect for an industrial-chic environment.
- Wooden kitchens with a timeless charm and a retro flavor.

- Kitchens in innovative and technological materials, such as Corian.
- Laminate kitchens are the cheapest, most versatile, and most practical ever.
- Masonry kitchens are rustic and characteristic of recreating the atmosphere of the country houses of the past.

How to design the kitchen: styles and costs

Designing a kitchen has costs that vary a lot according to the materials, as we have just seen, while regarding the styles we can find different price ranges, one for each budget. Choosing a modern, classic, country, shabby chic, or industrial kitchen does not affect the cost of the final kitchen because, for every style, there are finishes, appliances, taps, and details of every price range.

However, the type of composition can affect the kitchen budget: there are significant differences between a linear kitchen, the cheapest of all, a corner kitchen, one with a peninsula, and a kitchen with an island, which requires a more economical investment.

Finally, choosing a fitted or modular kitchen certainly has lower prices than a kitchen designed and built piece by piece by a carpenter. In this second case, the cost of the kitchen will be higher because the craftsmanship is infinitely longer and more accurate.

Renovating the kitchen or creating it from scratch: the importance of design

When you decide to design a kitchen, prices can also change according to need: is it about making some changes to renovate an existing kitchen, or is it time to create it from scratch?

The professional you choose certainly has an important task in this second case. He must define the perfect optimization of the spaces and advise you on choosing materials, colors, and composition.

How to modernize a classic kitchen instead? If you have decided to give a new and lively touch to your traditional kitchen, you can paint the furniture in a different color, change the tiles and floor or insert the latest generation appliances in place of the old ones; even change the taps and handles can give modernity to a classic kitchen without completely distorting it.

And how to modernize the kitchen worktop? There are professionals who make custom kitchen tops: you have to choose the material and the color, and the top will be cut according to the exact measurements of your kitchen and placed in the place of the old one. It is not too expensive and easy to make expedient to give a new face to an outdated kitchen.

Why design the kitchen with a professional: design and optimization

When you decide how to design your kitchen, many questions should be asked, but few ask themselves because they are not professionals in the trade. In this way, we neglect fundamental aspects and find ourselves with cuisine that does not meet our needs and does not meet our style and tastes. But what are these questions to ask?

How to organize the kitchen? This is a fundamental question to ask before proceeding with the work because the distribution of spaces significantly affects the functionality and practicality of your kitchen.

How to furnish the kitchen? Also, in this case, the professional will investigate your habits and lifestyle to identify which furniture you cannot miss and which you can easily do without.

Then there are even more particular situations, such as those who want to renovate the kitchen or wonder how to modernize a classic kitchen. In all these cases, having the support of a professional in the sector is essential to obtain a result that satisfies you both in terms of style, functionality, and space optimization.

Cucina is the brand most loved by Italians at any price. However, if you decide to design the kitchen, you will know that prices vary depending on your brand. Famous and renowned brands offer more complex solutions that inevitably require a greater economic investment. In contrast, other brands allow you to create tailor-made kitchens at affordable prices without sacrificing quality.

In fact, in the 2019 Budget Law, it is stated that the expenses admitted to the restructuring bonus are all ordinary and extraordinary maintenance interventions and restoration and conservative rehabilitation carried out on the individual real estate units. Therefore, you can recover 50% of the expenses incurred by presenting the necessary documentation. If you have decided that the time has come to design the kitchen, prices are certainly a factor that you cannot overlook: it is an important investment, and it is good that you take the time to make the right choice.

127

HERE ARE 20 IDEAS AND SUGGESTIONS ON HOW TO PLACE LIGHT POINTS IN THE KITCHEN.

— ◆◇◆ —

Modern And Classic Lighting

Lighting with spotlights

Like all the other rooms in our home, lighting in the kitchen, where we spend a lot of time, plays a very important role. Artificial light must be calibrated with the natural light present during the day to avoid the risk of placing an excessive number of lamps inside the room.

Beyond this aspect, we will have to consider that on the one hand, the chandeliers, ceiling lights, or wall lights that you choose to buy will illuminate the environment making it more functional, operational, and welcoming, but you must also remember that this will actively contribute to being an own real piece of furniture that will enrich the aesthetics of the kitchen.

These systems must also have unnecessary or simple maintenance (such as periodic cleaning), very high energy savings made possible thanks to LED technology, and very long life.

For these reasons, I have chosen to write a guide full of examples and advice on choosing the best solutions by bringing you concrete examples and images so that you can graphically visualize the final result (varying between different options and styles to try to embrace all types of requirement). I will also advise you on where and what products to buy, choosing the most reliable and suitable ones to complete this guide.

To do this, we will distinguish between the different parts of the kitchen to provide more ideas depending on the area you want to furnish, distinguishing between functional lights such as the cooking area and countertops. Work, decorative for the proper enhancement of the room and the environment to achieve a balanced degree of lighting.

Kitchen with retro vintage pendant lights

Ideas and advice

If the style of your kitchen is projected to be vintage or you love the retro style with warm, relaxing, and enveloping colors to illuminate the dining table, to relax while you eat, or to chat, these are the most suitable type of lights.

These systems precisely illuminate the tops and tables on which they are placed, so you could also choose to use them above hobs and those dedicated to preparation by changing the color of the light from warm to cold white.

It is also perfect for furnishing styles with high ceilings where a spotlight or a chandelier would not be able to concentrate the light optimally because they are too distant or where you want to obtain a more open and light effect without placing a large or bulky lighting system. If you prefer a more modern style, these pendant lights are more suited to the innovative style.

Kitchen design

A similar product for more modern projected furnishing styles.

Led Spotlights For Kitchens

Lighting with spotlights for the kitchen with an elegant and modern style, directional and adjustable LED spotlights are the best solution when you want to direct the light in a well-defined direction. For example, you can direct the light towards your worktop or the dining table. Discover the product used in the photo, which is also available in the black version.

Also available in the version with remote control to change color and light intensity. If you prefer to place just one spotlight, you can view the following product.

Modern spotlight

If you prefer a recessed spotlight for plasterboard, you can choose this model. Instead, spotlights in the modern kitchen led illuminate.

- o As an alternative, you might like a cleaner and more sober style, without pendant lamps or chandeliers. In this case, you can decide to set up your light points using the recessed LED spotlights that allow a more optimal and widespread diffusion compared to a single system oriented on a specific point.
- o Beyond this important aspect, these can be oriented towards the points in which we want to obtain a greater concentration of light, both for tastes in terms of furniture and for the functionality of the light that will be oriented in the point where we need it most, and diffused in the surrounding environment.
- o The last aspect to consider is that we can standardize different spaces. For example, if our kitchen were open to other environments, such as the hall, we could make the two different rooms more fluid and connected without interrupting our interior style.

o You can choose this product which also guarantees the possibility of directing the light to the desired points.

The only exception could be if the ceiling in your room were made of wooden beams. In this case, it would be better to choose a suspension lamp with spotlights to intervene with masonry work directly on the ceiling.

In this case, you can use cables and supports to be hooked to the beams to fix them safely, effectively illuminating your island or peninsula. Lights to illuminate the island and the counter.

Industrial Industrial Style

Perfect to effectively illuminate the table or the island of the room and create a seductive atmosphere, refined with a retro vintage 50s style; you can choose to use industrial lamps.

In this case, we will have to contribute to the functionality of our island by illuminating the surfaces in a targeted manner while maintaining a sober and orderly style, integrating perfectly with the existing lighting.

The choice of using a chandelier or industrial lamps also guarantees the characteristic of being able to illuminate the surrounding space, thus limiting the need for additional lights except in points where there is a particular need.

- Retro and vintage industrial lighting kitchen
- Vintage style island counter
- Counter lighting
- Applique

You can also decide to place a single lamp on the table to get a nostalgic retro 50's style.

Spherical lights

We can choose to illuminate our table and kitchen top with two beautiful sphere lamps as in the photo. Very modern, neat, and elegant style, combined with recessed spotlights on false ceilings.

In the pendant lights, we could then mount dimmable LED bulbs to be able to adjust the intensity according to the task we have to carry out, more intense during the work of preparing food and more relaxing when we are about to eat or chat with friends and relatives. If you like this style, here are some ideas and proposals. Then, click on the item you like the most in this style.

- Lights for kitchens
- Modern lamp
- Lights with suspensions
- Modern ornamental pendant lamps
- Ornamental pendants

If your kitchen is very large and you prefer a lighting style that is both decorative and functional, and effective, you can choose pendant lamps in a modern ornamental style.

- Diffused and concentrated light
- Technics and solutions

Color contrast effect

Contrasting the pendant lights with the color of the kitchen is another great idea. Although, in this case, I chose to combine a black lighting system with a white room, I could have done the same thing by placing a white lamp in a predominantly dark kitchen.

Contrast

Here is the product used to furnish this environment, supported by some spotlights that illuminate the house's perimeter.

Diffused light effect chandeliers

If modern style is what you are looking for and you want to focus a single lamp on the dining table, here are some innovative ideas you could use. For example, a single chandelier may not be necessary to illuminate the whole environment effectively; you could install spotlights near the corners or the perimeter of the kitchen to illuminate the most shaded points, while a chandelier may be placed above a table counter or a peninsula could be an excellent solution.

If, on the other hand, you choose a chandelier with more diffused light with a wider radius (such as the product of the image below), this could also reach the necessary areas and points, thus limiting the positioning of more lighting systems without intervening on the ceiling.

In addition to this indispensable function, the chandelier actively contributes to furnishing our interior, directly impacting the aesthetics and design of the kitchen itself.

Ring shape lamp

In this case, you have to choose a modern ring chandelier with natural light, so it is relaxing to enjoy a good dinner with family or friends and for moments of reading and study.

- How to illuminate kitchens
- Elegant applique
- Elegant wall lights on how to light up

An additional form of directional light is certainly LED or wall lamps that allow a better concentration of light on specific points. Here is a recommended product if you like this style. Discover also all the wall and wall lamps.

Spotlight for kitchen

Ideas and tips for under-cabinet lighting

One of the darkest areas of the kitchen is the under cabinet, both for reasons of arrangement of the shelves and furnishings and for the structure of the kitchen itself. In this case, we can also choose different solutions according to our personal preferences.

A few years ago, small neon ceiling lights were usually installed here, which illuminated the dining area's most hidden and shaded areas, obscured by the furniture and shelves.

At this point, we should use suitable lights, preferring LED ones over neon to obtain greater energy savings and a longer life span of the LED bulb itself. Both very thin LED strips placed at the perimeter of our shelves or in a central position can be chosen, and small LED ceiling lights will replace the old neon ones.

In this case, the light will have to highlight the work surface to encourage greater attention, choosing light bulbs with cold or natural light that stimulates greater concentration. Here we can choose to place a possible coffee machine, the cutting board, or a possible robot or mixer if the height of the shelves allows it.

In this example, the under-cabinet has been illuminated thanks to LED strip strips, which guarantee excellent lighting, very low consumption compared to the old and obsolete neon, last much longer, and are available with 230v 12 and 24v voltage.

- Illuminate under cabinet
- Under-cabinet lights

The LED strips can also illuminate the perimeters of islands and peninsulas, obtaining an almost futuristic effect. You can see a kitchen decorated with multicolored RGB stripes in the example, e.g., strip to illuminate under shelves, wardrobes, and shelves.

Illuminate the cooking area and hood

Certainly, not least is the arrangement of the lighting in the area where we physically cook our dishes, where we usually also find a possible hood connected to an air extractor that brings unwanted odors out of our room but also allows us to see at a glance whether the cooking level of the food. Also, in this case, we can use adjustable spotlights to be directed toward the kitchenette, or use the LED strips, thus exploiting the advantages of the LED.

Kitchen hood area

The light inside wardrobes, cabinets, and shelves lighting inside drawers. Another innovative idea is to use LED strips to illuminate the interior of the shelves, cabinets, cabinets, and our kitchen shelves, the most "hidden" places where we store utensils such as forks, pots, plates, glasses, and food.

This can be easily found where the cutlery or other objects are stored inside the drawers. The LED technology also allows us a very limited absorption, a very prolonged duration, and greater efficiency while limiting consumption to a few watts.

When we talk about interior decoration, two fundamental elements are the finish and color of the floors and walls. So let's see how to combine walls and floor, never going wrong and obtaining a unique and special effect in all house rooms.

The finish and color of floors and walls are two essential elements for defining any room. They act as a basis for the overall combination of the colors of the environment. We often find wooden floors in light, medium, and dark shades or traditional tile floors.

These two options, apparently so simple, however, have the possibility of being declined in a multitude of different solutions. Therefore, it is possible to opt for an incredible number of wall-floor combinations, depending on the style you have chosen and your tastes.

Wood, for example, can be shiny and smooth or opaque and with a very structured finish. Therefore, choosing the right parquet shade for your home already means giving a well-defined imprint to any room. The one that will lead you to choose a color for the walls rather than another will derive from this choice.

Modern floors

Therefore, it is very important to have clear, right from the start, what tone you want to give to the environment so as not to obtain unexpected results that are not very similar to your idea of home.

- How to match walls and floor: some suggestions
- Focus on light and dark contrast
- Choose neutral colors
- Choose shades that are part of the same palettes
- How to match walls and floor
- How to match walls and floor

Whether your home is new and therefore you are organizing it for the first time, or you are about to redecorate it because you want to give it a breath of fresh air, you will still find yourself faced with the problem of having to choose the tone to give to the space and therefore how to match walls and floors.

You will certainly have more choices if you have to start from scratch. On the other hand, if the floor is already defined, you will have to start from this to define the walls. If the walls are already defined, the floor will have to adapt.

If your intention is, however, to change the floor, which is the most complex intervention, then you will still find yourself in a situation like the initial one, in which you will have the opportunity to rethink the decoration of your home from scratch.

Focus on light and dark contrast

1. If you are looking for a strong effect, which is impactful for those who enter the room, then focus on the contrast between dark and light colors. For example, the floor can be dark and the walls light or vice versa: the effect you will get will certainly be unique.
2. The dark floors are combined with a light wall, while the light floors illuminate an environment with dark

walls. Do not forget that when the walls are light, the room will appear brighter and wider due to the optical effect that the lighter shades cause, but it could make the room seem too large and dispersed. At this point, a dark floor will help balance the spaces, making the room more welcoming.

- Choose neutral colors
- By choosing neutral colors for the walls, you will have a sober background in perfect continuity with any type of furniture and any floor finish. The most popular neutral colors for the walls are gray, cream, white and taupe, but there are many that can adapt to any environment and style

Neutral shades with warm undertones match perfectly with warm wooden floors or tiles in warm tones. Neutral walls with cool undertones, on the other hand, are clearly to be combined with floors with the same undertone, both in wood and in tiles.

Advice

Choose shades that are part of the same palettes. To choose which wall color to match the color of the floor, use the color palettes available everywhere on the internet. In addition, you can bet on the color schemes that Pantone, the well-known leader in the color industry, provides.

In this way, you will be sure to match the right colors without combining shades that do not agree and would create an out-of-tune and disharmonious effect. Instead, use color schemes, juxtaposing them to see what they look like when paired so that you can imagine them in your home.

Floors with orange undertones, for example, look great when paired with those from the blue family. The floors in the many variations of red, from cherry to vermilion, are perfect with greens. Light-colored floors, for example, yellow, go very well with purple walls. It's a simple and fun way to find the right palettes for every room in your home.

145

HOW TO COMBINE WALLS-AND FLOORS

———— ◆◇◆ ————

How to combine walls and floors can be fun and straightforward if you follow the right steps. We have summarized them to make your choice more serene and aware. The decoration of your home starts from knowing how to combine walls and floors with taste and style. Here is a roundup of images that show you how.

Great appliances

Proportion is the basis of the design. Each object contained within a space must be related to the size of the neighboring one to generate a balance of shape. For example, a large piece, whether a fridge, a piece of furniture or a painting, in a small space would make the whole environment seem disorganized, causing the entire interior project to collapse.

Too many colors and patterns

To combine colors and patterns, you have to be good! If you get away with mixes, use them thoughtfully in your small kitchen, but be careful not to overdo it by combining materials and designs that do not interact with each other. Inside the visual cone, there is a point called fire. Our eye lingers, capable of reading a precise area in a matter of seconds, and therefore all the objects contained within, relating each material and shape to the neighboring one.

Disorder

Eliminate any useless object; everything will be visible instantly once you enter the kitchen. Put each piece on the shelves or in the drawers, and leave only a few pieces visible, which identify your style; you can change them later and convey a sense of immediate order.

Ideas

- 1 Locate the functional triangle
- Ergonomics is the discipline that works on the relationship between the functions that people

perform through objects with which they interact, with the aim of identifying the most suitable solutions for carrying out the work. For example, the room used as a kitchen is heavily based on ergonomics, so we speak of a "work triangle." By connecting the position of the refrigerator, stove, and washing machine, we frequently draw a fictitious geometry. Attention to this aspect comes from the functionality of small spaces. Within this shape, we must move freely.

In closed spaces, it is always better to design with elements that recall the shape of the letters P, C, or G; in open spaces, the linear or island versions work better, while for passing corridors, parallel solutions.

Group the objects

The countertop is vital when cooking, and tidy space is certainly more comfortable and pleasing to the eye. Gather jars, accessories, and objects in a single space, at most two, so that everything is more practical, with areas equipped to perform the function. For example, the preparation area can be close to the shelves of the jars, the cleaning area to a free shelf, and the socialization area to the cabinet on which you store plates and glasses. You could display your cups or plates on open shelves and let the objects give the room a style! Even a portion of the wall, apparently insignificant, can be important and be equipped orderly.

A peninsula as a table

People often tell me, "I would like, but I can't," and the challenge starts, and the project that goes beyond the ideal dimension begins. The peninsula or the island is one of those spaces that have always been so desired, but people are afraid of the space that it is feared that it may unnecessarily subtract. But, especially in small kitchens, where functions are grouped, the multifunctional hob is essential; it is a wild card: a worktop, support surface, table, or place of exchange where you can also have a coffee on the go.

Tone-on-tone walls and kitchen

Color is vital even in small spaces, especially if you are not a total white fanatic. Using it unevenly, for example, with darker wall units than the base units, can be a valid choice, but the "stain" effect, which is often desired, is guaranteed. On the other hand, especially if the four walls are short, using a single color for the walls and kitchen can be advantageous. It blends the two elements, creating the illusion of an entire expanding space, making the room more pleasant.

Neutral and bright colors

The light shades charm the kitchen design and go well with any material. It is the color most chosen by Italians. It adapts to any pre-existing furniture, color, and architecture because it has no impact and has the "ability" to adapt to both a minimalist and a classic style. Just think of the doors with wooden frames or those reflecting glass.

To add a more whimsical touch to the environment, you can combine a more sophisticated worktop in darker tones or work with metals, lights, or accessories.

Niches and containers

Do you know those unused, lifeless spaces? Focus them and make them functional by designing custom-made shelves, open or closed by flush-to-the-wall opaque or glass doors, with a 1950s flavor.

In addition to giving a place to the equipment usually placed on the top, you will transform the uneven walls and the cantilevered volumes into smooth, equipped walls.

The kitchen is usually the most intimate and welcoming environment in your home. To experience it to the fullest, it is important not to leave anything to chance; only in this way will you create the right kitchen for you.

Everything you need to know about a kitchen designer

The kitchen is one of the spaces in a home where people spend a lot of time. This is one of the reasons why kitchens need to be designed with proper thinking and planning. Efficiency, practicality, and aesthetics are important considerations when designing a kitchen.

Hiring a kitchen designer to ensure all your important considerations are well taken care of is good. But is it worth the investment? Can the kitchen designer complete the task on time and within budget?

Like all professionals, kitchen designers also have their reputation at stake and would not shy away from their commitments. However, a functional and efficient kitchen can save you time and energy and add it to your working hours. So the investment is worth it. Plus, your kitchen will last longer. You should consider hiring a kitchen designer to give your kitchen a more eye-catching look and make it more comfortable and efficient.

CERTIFIED KITCHEN DESIGNER, WHO IS A KITCHEN DESIGNER?

---◆◇◆---

- A kitchen designer is a certified professional who works alongside experts in other fields such as interior designers and material manufacturers and ultimately comes up with the best design plans for your kitchen. These days, people don't bother hiring these experts for their invaluable assistance. However, you may still think they're not worth hiring. For a more balanced and informed view, read on.

Let's see now why you should hire a kitchen designer.

Why should you hire a kitchen designer?

Certified kitchen designers are professionals who come up with unique design ideas for kitchens. They have a strong background of experts from various fields such as interior designers, architects, engineers, and product manufacturers. So even if you end up spending huge bucks on hiring one, they can ensure greater kitchen efficiency, giving you a long-term economic advantage.

What does a kitchen designer do?

- They reach out to potential customers and try to understand their expectations.
- Next, these experts explain to them what might be the best designs that suit their needs.
- They can explain why a particular idea may or may not be suitable.
- They can also complete the job within a limited time frame.
- After detailed sessions with experts from different sectors, they organize a simulation session for their clients.
- Modular kitchen design

Benefits

Build your modular kitchen with the advice of these experts; you can make your dreams come true. With the assistance of experts from various fields, you can get an impromptu version of your intended goal.

Modern and innovative design ideas

They can bring forth innovative kitchen designs, such as modular kitchen designs. Compared to custom kitchen designs, these are known for their low budget. Plus, since these are designed and made in bulk, they can be inexpensive. In addition, the cabinets that fit into the modular kitchen design can be moved and placed anywhere you choose. They also offer you a wide range of selections.

Better preservation

The kitchen requires a lot of space to store a large number of kitchen items such as glasses, plates, tiles, and crockery. Hence, these kitchen designers can help you find a range of attractive cabinet designs that offer better storage. This can create a kitchen environment where the essentials are readily available, saving time and energy that you may have spent searching for randomly arranged materials.

Improved flooring, ventilation, and lighting

It is necessary to have good air circulation in your kitchen, to avoid retaining the smell of the different dishes prepared in the kitchen. You also need to have quality lighting in your kitchen. The type of flooring you choose for your kitchen can also determine the brightness of your kitchen. Choosing a light-colored floor can make the kitchen brighter.

The best design ideas

They can offer you a range of the best designs and products available, such as the best flooring options, the best built-in stove models, and other built-in appliances like dishwashers.

Within your budget

They can offer you the best products which are also affordable. This means you get the best services within your budget. What more could you ask for!

- Custom kitchen design
- Disadvantages
- Initial expenses to hire a kitchen designer

One of the major drawbacks of hiring a kitchen designer is the initial investment you need to make. However, it's worth it in the long run. The increased efficiency of appliances and other materials such as cabinets and floors can help you save money you might have spent on repairing or replacing the cheapest products available.

You risk hiring a designer with limited experience. However, before hiring one, you need to do quality research on the best kitchen designers available on the market. Hiring an inexperienced designer can leave you with bad cooking for the rest of your life. That's why hiring certified professionals in this field are the safest option. They have the knowledge, experience, and connections with the people of the industry. These factors are important to your kitchen project.

CONCLUSION

———— ◆◇◆ ————

The advantages and disadvantages of hiring a certified kitchen designer. You are now able to decide what might be best for you. You can see that the advantages far outweigh the disadvantages. They carry forward the innovative ideas available, such as modular kitchen design. Moreover, these designs have proven to be the best and most affordable compared to custom kitchen designs.

Having a kitchen designer design your kitchen is a really good option. However, it is the best choice for people who have a busy schedule as these efficient kitchens can help them save time and energy.

Basic stages of kitchen remodeling

Few home remodeling projects bring more benefits and headaches than a major kitchen remodel job. If you hire a general contractor to handle a major job that expands the kitchen footprint, costs can easily enter the six-figure range. However, if you have the courage to tackle the job on your own, the job could take many months to complete, and you may have to live without a kitchen for a good portion of that time.

But a sparkling new kitchen will make your home more livable and increase the value of your real estate assets like few other remodeling projects can. In addition, a new large kitchen will be at the center of family life and can be the center of social gatherings. A fully remodeled kitchen is a project worth the time, money, and effort. You can avoid being overwhelmed if you fully understand the steps that go into the process before you begin.

Assess needs and wants

A large number of kitchen remodeling projects end up disappointing a homeowner or shocking him with the cost simply because he didn't take the time to determine what he wanted and what he could afford.

Needs versus desires in a kitchen remodel

Start by asking yourself what persistent problems you are having with your current kitchen. Is it a question of having little space to cook effectively? Too little space to store food and dishes? Do you miss the dining areas? Are the appliances ineffective or too old? Or does the kitchen make you wince because it's so dated and ugly?

Prioritize a list of the things you would like in your new kitchen, ranked by their importance. It is helpful to distinguish between the items you need and those you simply want.

Reshape reality check

In the initial planning phase, tackle the two-part reality of a kitchen remodel project: the logistics of the job itself and the expenses involved. For example, if subcontractors managed by a general contractor does the work, you will have strangers following you around the house and making noise and confusion for a few weeks or maybe even a couple of months. But, on the other hand, if you're planning on doing the work yourself, will your kitchen downtime likely be much more extended, and do you have the time and DIY skills to do it?

The resale value of the kitchen remodel

Consider paying back a new kitchen. If you plan to stay in your home for many years, a dream kitchen may be worth the high cost as it will serve as a functional and attractive family space for decades.

But if you're an empty nester who plans to downsize into a smaller home over the next five years, perhaps a surface-level kitchen remodel is the most practical option. A kitchen is a very personal space, and your idea of a dream kitchen may not resemble the idea of the next owner. Kitchen remodels often return a good portion of their cost into better home equity, but not all of it.

Be prepared for a compromise

From the beginning of the planning phase, establish a mindset willing to look for ways to cut costs on your kitchen remodel project. For example, the easiest and most expensive way to remodel a kitchen is to offload most of the planning, design, and management of workers to a general contractor. But the contractor comes at a significant cost, and you can save a lot of money if you're willing to serve as your contractor and hire and supervise individual subcontractors to do the practical work.

Additionally, your cost savings will be greatly magnified if you are willing and able to tackle certain tasks independently. Prepare to compromise on the materials of your new kitchen. It's easy to get dreamy eyes about custom cabinetry and marble floor tile, but you'll find that there are hardwood veneer cabinetry and mass-produced porcelain floor tile that will also look great. Is this restaurant gas range necessary, or will a good quality consumer range do? You might even consider using reclaimed cabinets and other materials to create a unique yet affordable vintage kitchen look if you're creative.

Kitchen design and planning

With a realistic idea of what you need in a new kitchen and a mindset of certain flexibility, you can start brainstorming and developing a concrete and achievable plan for your new kitchen.

Basic kitchen countertops

While you have a wide range of possibilities, use one of the five classic kitchen design floors. For ease of movement, all the tops represent some form of that classic workflow model, the kitchen triangle.

- One wall design

-Design of the corridor

-L-shaped design

-Double L design

-U-shaped design

One of these classic kitchen design countertops will be the logical choice for your new kitchen. From there, you can peruse a number of resources to help develop actual designs and projects for your kitchen:

Kitchen Design Software: Cheap online or free kitchen design software helps you with the difficult task of space planning.

Physical Design Packages: These kits have cardboard punch-outs representing cabinets and appliances. Placing punch-outs on a kitchen grill helps you realistically visualize the space available.

Kitchen Designers: Kitchen designers at home improvement companies or kitchen design stores typically design your kitchen for free. However, they will guide you to their suppliers and their work teams.

Independent designers will have the most freedom and may give you the best product because they have fewer restrictions. However, they will charge you for their services, either by the hour or a percentage of the project's cost.

General Contractors: The GCs themselves who manage kitchen remodeling projects may be able to assist you in the early stages of kitchen planning, although their design assistance won't be detailed until you hire them. But most GCs bidding on a job will offer suggestions and perhaps even plan sketches as part of their proposals. So even just talking to contractors can help you clarify your plans.

Hire a contractor or do it yourself

Whether you've created your kitchen project yourself or worked with a design professional, once you've chosen a kitchen layout and developed the designs, it's time to decide who you will hire to transform those ideas into reality. There are three options:

Hire a general contractor (GC). These are generally construction/construction companies specializing in managing large projects from start to finish. They can range from small companies with two or three people to large companies with dozens of employees. In large companies, the commission charged by the GC ranges from 15 to 25 percent of the total labor cost.

GCs are often owner/operator businesses. The owner can do a good deal of the work himself, possibly one or two staff carpenters, then subcontract specialized work, such as wiring, plumbing, and tile installation. A well-experienced owner/operator contractor is an excellent choice for a kitchen remodel project as their overhead costs are generally much lower than larger companies. In addition, these smaller contractors usually don't charge a fee, as their costs are calculated in the overall job estimates.

Do it yourself. You are doing all the practical work yourself at the other end of the ladder. This is a practical alternative if you are a very experienced DIYer, perfectly informed in all the required skills, and if you have a lot of free time to do the job.

But this is not an option for the faint of heart because the kitchen remodel is a big project. It is not uncommon for a do-it-yourself who undergoes a major kitchen renovation to find himself a whole year in a project with the end still months away. However, a good DIY can cut your project costs by doing all the work.

Physical Design Packages: These kits have cardboard punch-outs representing cabinets and appliances. Placing punch-outs on a kitchen grill helps you realistically visualize the space available.

Kitchen Designers: Kitchen designers at home improvement companies or kitchen design stores typically design your kitchen for free. However, they will guide you to their suppliers and their work teams.

Independent designers will have the most freedom and may give you the best product because they have fewer restrictions. However, they will charge you for their services, either by the hour or a percentage of the project's cost.

General Contractors: The GCs themselves who manage kitchen remodeling projects may be able to assist you in the early stages of kitchen planning, although their design assistance won't be detailed until you hire them. But most GCs bidding on a job will offer suggestions and perhaps even plan sketches as part of their proposals. So even just talking to contractors can help you clarify your plans.

Do it yourself. You are doing all the practical work yourself at the other end of the ladder. This is a practical alternative if you are a very experienced DIYer, perfectly informed in all the required skills, and if you have a lot of free time to do the job.

But this is not an option for the faint of heart because the kitchen remodel is a big project. It is not uncommon for a do-it-yourself who undergoes a major kitchen renovation to find himself a whole year in a project with the end still months away. However, a good DIY can cut your project costs in half by doing all the work and mandatory inspections for authorization requirements. The inspector will examine the installation while the wall surfaces are still removed to ensure that it has been performed according to the code. If you have done this work yourself, it is your responsibility to organize the inspection.

Approximate wiring

As complex as the plumbing system, the electrical service updates for a major kitchen renovation could be more extensive. Modern kitchens have very heavy electrical loads, and the code can take up to seven circuits or more. Therefore, your home should be serviced with at least 200 amps to effectively power a large, modern kitchen. Unfortunately, this means that many kitchen remodeling projects require an electrician to update the entire electrical service of the house.

As the electrician conducts the new circuits in the kitchen, he will likely abandon any existing wiring to run new cables for all the kitchen circuits. But, again, the approximate installation of the wiring will have to be reviewed and approved by the inspector before the project can move on to the next stage.

HVAC Rough-In

While not always necessary, any new HVAC ductwork required by the project is done concurrently with completing the wiring and plumbing work. The installation of sheet metal ducts is usually performed by an HVAC contractor who understands the physics of airflow. It can position the new ventilation, and cold air return registers in the most effective positions.

Wall and ceiling finishing

With the next step, the kitchen will transition from a battle zone to something that looks like a kitchen. Once the plumbing, wiring, and HVAC works have been completed and passed by the inspector, the walls and ceilings can be closed. Next, the external walls will be insulated with fiberglass to provide a buffer between the kitchen and the elements. With accessible wall cavities, this is a good time to install high-quality insulation.

Next, the drywall is hung, and the seams are taped and finished. Walls and ceilings are now primed and painted. If the ceilings are textured, the texture is now applied.

Insulation, drywall installation, and priming and finishing of walls and ceilings are all activities that homeowners can do on their own to save money. However, remember that professionals can get this job done very quickly and are relatively inexpensive.

Install the flooring

The floor installation is one of the last stages before installing cabinets, appliances, and devices. It is normally kept until the end to avoid the wear of the new flooring.

If a general contractor manages the project, his flooring subcontractors will arrive to carry out the installation. The time required (and the expense) will depend on the type of flooring you have chosen.

Vinyl sheet is the least expensive flooring choice and can usually be laid in a day. Do-it-yourselfers can do this job, but professional installation is not very expensive since the required work time is not great.

The ceramic tile requires a concrete support board base, to which the tile is glued with thin-set mortar. The tile is then grouted. Professional installation can be expensive, even with inexpensive tiles, due to the extensive work required. However, do-it-yourselfers capable and willing to do this job can enjoy good cost savings.

Engineered wood looks like solid wood (its surface finish is real wood), but it is much less expensive. In addition, the tongue and groove planks are relatively easy for DIYers to install. Laminate flooring is a very popular choice for kitchens due to its low price and ease of installation. However, some shapes are not recommended for humid places such as kitchens. Nevertheless, laminate planks are easy to install for DIYers.

Solid wood: hardwood is less popular because water can deform it if it is not dried quickly. However, it is a viable choice for the kitchen with proper care. Installers can lay the wood on a medium-sized kitchen floor in three days. Unfortunately, installing hardwood floors yourself is a very difficult DIY project.

Install cabinets and countertops

As the kitchen remodel draws close, finishing carpenters will install the cabinets and countertops. Hanging a piece of furniture requires patience. Your local furniture supplier should have work teams that can hang your cabinets, usually for a day or two. Any competent carpenter can do this job if you subcontract the job, or you can do it yourself, although you will need helpers to do it.

While it sounds easy enough, installing countertops is more difficult than it looks. Ceramic tile countertops are probably best installed by tile professionals who might also install ceramic tile flooring. Suppose you use artificial materials, such as Silestone, Formica, or Corian. In that case, you may not even have the do-it-yourself installation option, as these materials are difficult to purchase even for do-it-yourselfers.

These solid surface materials must be manufactured and installed by licensed manufacturers affiliated with the manufacturers. Countertops in granite, marble, and synthetic quartz are so heavy that the best option is to have them installed by the shop that manufactured them to your specifications.

Since false ceilings must be installed perfectly flat and level, a good installation depends on perfectly level bases and solidly anchored

Install appliances, plumbing, and wiring

You are on the penultimate lap: installing household appliances and final plumbing and lighting systems connections. The appliances are delivered and put in place, and the plumber returns to connect the dishwasher and the refrigerator water supply and install and connect the sink and taps. The electrician also returns to install the lighting fixtures, connect switches and sockets, and install the piping covers.

Homeowners can do some or all of this work, but if the professionals were used for the earlier stages of the wiring and plumbing work, the final connections are normally part of the contracted work.

Inspection and completion

With all the remodeling tasks completed, now is the time for the finishing touches:

If you are working with a general contractor, make an overview and list all the details that do not completely satisfy your satisfaction. Discussing this punch list with your GC is a normal part of any remodeling project and includes things like molding joints that don't exactly fit and the repair of scars and dents on the walls.

During the appliance's installation, faucet handle covers and any important discrepancies that you may notice are not yet in place. So now is the time to make sure you are happy with all the work that has been done.

At the end of the project, your permits will need to be final, meaning the various inspectors will need to visit your kitchen, review the work, and stamp your permit application as final or complete. If you have worked with contractors, the required inspections will normally be arranged, but if you have done the work yourself, you are instructed to contact the inspectors to finalize the permits.

A good contractor employs a cleaner who specializes in cleaning buildings. So take a break and hire a cleaner to clean your kitchen if you do it yourself. And now, your cooking is done! So enjoy the new space and convenience and feel good about making one of the best home remodeling choices.

How to design a modular kitchen

To design a modular kitchen, we first need to know the standard sizes of the furniture that we will insert in this compartment. The kitchen is one of the most "technical" rooms in the house; to have good functionality, it is also necessary to know the minimum distances between one piece of furniture and another.

It is also necessary to know the minimum ergonomic spaces to move well in front of the different work surfaces. Finally, I will show you the characteristics of the different types of kitchens, starting from the classic linear composition and ending with the modern "island."

The components of a kitchen

To properly design a kitchen, you need to know the measurements of its components. So let's say that a kitchen cabinet mainly consists of the following three modules: bases, wall units, and columns.

These elements have standard measures, they are:

- Bases: (width = 60 cm; depth = 60 cm; height = 90 cm)
- Wall units: (width = 60 cm; depth = 30cm; height = 72/40 cm);
- Columns: (width = 60cm; depth = 60cm; height = 200cm).

However, it must be said that there may be minimal differences between brand and manufacturer brand.

Types of composition

The compositions obtained with the base units, the wall units, and the columns are different; they can be summarized in linear, corner, peninsula, and island arrangements.

The linear composition is the simplest, and when composing it, all you have to do is place the different modules next to each other. But, at the same time, the corner composition requires a particular module, a special piece, both for the base and the wall unit, is shaped so that the kitchen turns around the corner.

The peninsula composition must consider two more factors in the sizing of the composition. The first is the contemporaneity of the doors opening: a certain distance must be left between the two bases facing each other to ensure that the respective doors can open without getting in the way. The second is that of the minimum maneuvering space that a person occupies while standing while working in front of the table. Finally, the island composition generally uses deeper bases that can even exceed 100 centimeters in some cases.

How to create the kitchen island

Kitchen islands are a common accessory in modern kitchens. They have many functions, such as creating a much-needed workspace in open spaces to allow people to sit and eat in the kitchen without getting in the cook's way. Being often at the center of the kitchen, islands are very important and require careful planning that considers their purpose and aesthetics.

You don't need to be a carpenter to build an island, but you should have basic construction knowledge and familiarity with tools. By following these instructions, you will learn several methods for building and customizing a kitchen island.

1) Get two identical shelves: these should be about the same height as the counter or lower. They must be sturdy and preferably deeper than standard shelves. You can paint them before proceeding if you want them to have different colors. Measure the depth and width

2) Determine the size of the counter: decide how long the countertop should be. It should measure at least as much as the two shelves' depth, plus a few inches to create the counter's edge, but you can also insert up to one and a half meters of space between the two shelves. Then determine the width by measuring the depth of the shelves and adding a few inches for the edge.

3) Buy or build the counter: once you have the measurements, you can buy or build your counter. For

example, you can buy a board of MDF (Medium Density Particleboard) or any other material of the necessary size at a home improvement store.

- Glulam is a popular option because it is inexpensive, easy to clean, and suitable for kitchen use.
- Granite can also be an option, but as the slabs are very heavy, you need to allow less spacing between the two shelves to ensure the stand is stable.
- If you intend to build the counter yourself from an MDF board, you can paint it to make it look more like a table; alternatively, you can laminate or tile the surface to make it suitable for food preparation.

4) Secure the counter to the shelves: place the counter on the shelves, turn with the shelves facing out, and use brackets to secure it, screwing on the edges where the wood is thickest. Put some screws underneath as well. Use screws of the appropriate length to make sure they don't protrude. It will take more attention if you have decided to use a granite table because you cannot screw it on. Ask your nearest home improvement store for information before proceeding.

5) Make the finishes you want.: if you have used MDF wood, you can paint it, tile it, or laminate the surface

according to your needs and tastes. You can screw or glue hooks on the sides of the shelves to hang kitchen towels. You can put a bar with hooks to hang pots and pans using the proper fixings. Remember not to add too much weight not to strain the screws.

6) An alternative method can be to use a piece of furniture. For example, you can add a standard kitchen cabinet between the shelves if you want more storage space instead of legroom. This will also give the island more solid air, and you can hide the dishwasher and other appliances from view.

The cabinet must be the same height as the shelves for the counter to rest on all three pieces. Therefore, it is better to choose slightly lower shelves than the piece of furniture and then add some thicknesses. Furthermore, the cabinet must not be deeper than the two shelves.

1. The counter, therefore, must be as long as both the shelves and the cabinet, plus a few centimeters for the edge. So, again, the width of the counter will be the width of the two shelves.

2. Before screwing the table, screw the cabinet and shelves together from the inside. It is best to screw on the edges, as before, but this time on the horizontal dividers at the top and bottom, if you can

reach them. Then screw the cabinet to the table from below, always paying attention to the length of the screws that must not protrude from the opposite surface.

Use a desk or table

1) Find the right table or desk. You will need a table or desk with two flat sides to act as legs for this island. You can buy such a table at a furniture store or build it from two rectangles of solid wood or thick plywood. They must be at least 5 centimeters thick.

- The first rectangle will be the work surface and must be cut to the desired size. The second rectangle will be cut in half and used to create the table legs, shortening them if they are too tall. First, join these pieces by making a 45-degree cut on both sides of the countertop and one side of the legs. Then you will need to press these corners together by coating the inside of the joint with wood glue and screwing to the side, from the legs towards the center of the countertop, in at least four places.

- Once done, you can paint or laminate the outer sides of the island as you wish.

2) Get furniture and containers. You will need to secure various furniture and containers under the table to create usable spaces. The choice will be determined partly by the space available, as the width of the island will determine the depth of each cabinet and partly by your needs.

- You will need to make sure that the furniture's dimensions are the same as the width and length of the table. In addition, they must not be higher than the legs.
- Use a pair of wall units with shelves and join them together to maximize usable island space. Better if the cabinets are without dividers, so you can take the items stored on both sides.

3) Secure the cabinets to the table. Screw the cabinets from the inside to secure them to the island, and screw them together if the wood is thick enough.

* Make sure you use screws that reach halfway down the wood panel; otherwise, you risk creating cracks, deformations, or holes on the outer surface.

4) add details and finish. You can paint the cabinets using the same color as the workbench or contrasting color. You can also tile the surface and add glulam or a granite slab.

Use a chest of drawers

1) Get a chest of drawers. If you want to turn it into a kitchen island, it needs to be the right size. With drawers that are too long or heavy, you will get a modest result. Instead, try to find something roughly the same size as the area you want to occupy.

* If you want to paint the chest of drawers, the best time to do it is now because it will be more complicated after putting the work surface in it.

2) Add legs or wheels. If the surface of the chest of drawers is too low, you can make it the desired height by adding legs (for a fixed island), wheels (to make it mobile), or using both solutions. It also evaluates the thickness of the

countertop when calculating the height of the completed island.

* The most suitable method for adding legs or wheels depends on the features of the chest of drawers. Consult an expert and follow the instructions provided with the wheels or legs.

3) Replace the back, if necessary. If the back of the dresser is ugly or damaged, replace it with a cut-to-size MDF or chipboard board. Then, carefully remove the old piece and nail the new one.

* You can make the back of the cabinet more useful by coating it with chalkboard paint - you will create a surface on which to write a grocery list with chalk or for children to play.

* Alternatively, use this space to hang hooks or bars by placing sturdy crossbars on the other side of the back panel. You can hang towels, oven mitts, or kitchen tools.

4) Replace or re-coat the countertop. To have a worktop more suitable for food preparation, you can carefully remove the top table of the cabinet and replace it with a material of your choice. It shouldn't be difficult to tile if the existing surface is smooth, with straight, finished edges. Decide what to do based on your skills, needs, and tastes.

Use kitchen cabinets

1) Buy some kitchen furniture. Any combination of kitchen cabinets that don't already have a workbench will do. In this way, you can combine them in the configuration you prefer, completing the work with the plan. In addition, you can buy furniture similar to what you already have in the kitchen, or different furniture to combine as you like.

* Pay attention to the back and sides of the furniture. If they aren't finished, you'll have to do it yourself. Cover them with plywood or MDF boards which you can then paint.

2) Arrange the furniture in the order you prefer. You will probably have to join several pieces together. Do this by screwing in the furniture from the inside, using the structure areas where the wood is thickest.

> You can put furniture turned in the same direction, in opposite directions, or, if space permits, put a piece of furniture on its side. It depends on the result you are looking for and how you intend to use the space.

3) Add a surface. Once the furniture is in place, build or buy a work surface covering all the pieces. You can use different materials, from glulam to granite. Even a

concrete slab (colored, patterned, or raw) can work fine. It must have dimensions suitable for your chosen furniture; just make sure you leave a few extra inches in width and length for the counter's edge.

4) Do the finishes. Finally, refine the island by customizing it to your liking. You can modify it to match your style, kitchen, or home better. You can also add containers to maximize space on your work surface, creating more space for appliances or preparing fantastic family meals.

- You can paint the lower sections of your new island a contrasting color to the other furniture, or you can leave them as they are. Experiment with light colors to give the kitchen a pop touch, or use shades that recall existing colors in the kitchen, such as those of fruit or a vase in plain sight.

- Add elements to the sides or back of the furniture. For example, you can mount a paper roll holder or hooks for kitchen rags. You can put a magazine rack for recipes or cooking magazines. You can even put a container for the kitchen tools you use most. Most of these things will need to be screwed to the wood. Always make sure to fasten them in places that are thick enough to support the screw, for example, on the shelf support or the main structure of the island. You can also use strong glues suitable for hanging items.

Tips and tricks to always keep the kitchen tidy

Comfort and order are useful tips to keep the kitchen always tidy. How to organize and divide spaces functionally. To always keep the kitchen tidy, you need to take advantage of the height and the containers and eliminate what is superfluous. Here are some useful tips to make your kitchen tidy.

The kitchen is the beating heart of the house; together with the living room, it represents the place where you get together with family and friends to spend time together. Precisely this contributes to making the kitchen untidy, to avoid finding yourself in a similar situation, all you have to do is follow our advice.

When you cook, you get creative, so you use many tools, but there are some that you just don't need! As a result, the kitchen becomes the permanent home of many useless utensils accumulated over time, which only take up space.

Be careful, before taking all the objects and throwing them away, consider that you can donate them to those who need them, but they must certainly be in good condition! Choosing which items to get rid of means decluttering, then scouring the kitchen and figuring out which items you need and which ones you can easily do without.

You can think about collecting the items and asking questions:

- When did I use it?
- When could I use it?
- What could I use it for?

If these questions are answered negatively, you have to remove the objects and recover space; you can use it differently!

How to create the kitchen island

Kitchen islands are a common fixture in modern kitchens. They have many functions, such as creating a much-needed workspace in open spaces for people to sit and eat in the kitchen without getting in the cook's way. Being often at the center of the kitchen, islands are very important and require careful planning that considers their purpose and aesthetics.

You don't need to be a carpenter to build an island, but you should have basic construction knowledge and familiarity with tools. By following these instructions, you will learn several methods for building and customizing a kitchen island.

1) Get two identical shelves. These should be about the same height as the counter or just lower. They must be sturdy and preferably deeper than standard shelves. You can paint them before proceeding if you want them to have different colors. Measure the depth and width

2) Determine the size of the counter. First, decide how long the countertop should be. It should measure at least as much as the two shelves' depth, plus a few inches to create the counter's edge, but you can also insert up to one and a half meters of space between the two shelves. Then determine the width by measuring the depth of the shelves and adding a few inches for the edge.

3) Buy or build the counter. Once you have the measurements, you can buy or build your counter. You can buy a board of MDF (Medium Density Particleboard) or any other material of the necessary size at a home improvement store.

- Glulam is a popular option because it is inexpensive, easy to clean, and suitable for kitchen use.

- Granite can also be an option, but as the slabs are very heavy, you need to allow for less spacing between the two shelves to ensure the stand is stable.

If you intend to build the counter yourself from an MDF board, you can paint it to make it look more like a table; alternatively, you can laminate or tile the surface to make it suitable for food preparation.

4) Secure the counter to the shelves. Place the counter on the shelves, turn with the shelves facing out, and use brackets to secure it, screwing on the edges where the wood is thickest. Put some screws underneath as well. Use screws of the appropriate length to make sure they don't protrude.

- It will take more attention if you have decided to use a granite table because you cannot screw it on. Ask your nearest home improvement store for information before proceeding.

5) Make the finishes you want. If you have used MDF wood, you can paint it, tile it, or laminate the surface according to your needs and tastes. In addition, you can screw or glue hooks on the sides of the shelves to hang

kitchen towels using the hardware. Suitable, you can put a bar with hooks to hang pots and pans. Remember not to add too much weight not to strain the screws.

6) An alternative method can be to use a piece of furniture. For example, you can add a standard kitchen cabinet between the shelves if you want more storage space instead of legroom. This will also give the island more solid air, and you can hide the dishwasher and other appliances from view.

The cabinet must be the same height as the shelves for the counter to rest on all three pieces. Therefore, it is better to choose slightly lower shelves than the piece of furniture and then add some thicknesses. Furthermore, the cabinet must not be deeper than the two shelves.

- The counter, therefore, must be as long as both the shelves and the cabinet, plus a few centimeters for the edge. So, again, the width of the counter will be the width of the two shelves.
- Before screwing the table, screw the cabinet and shelves together from the inside. It is best to screw on the edges, as before, but this time on the horizontal dividers at the top and bottom, if you can reach them. Then screw the cabinet to the table from below, always paying attention to the length

of the screws that must not protrude from the opposite surface.

Use a desk or table

1) Find the right table or desk. You will need a table or desk with two flat sides to act as legs for this island. You can buy such a table at a furniture store or build it from two rectangles of solid wood or thick plywood. They must be at least 5 centimeters thick.

- The first rectangle will be the work surface and must be cut to the desired size. The second rectangle will be cut in half and used to create the table legs, shortening them if they are too tall. Join these pieces by making a 45-degree cut on both sides of the countertop and one side of the legs. Then you will need to press these corners together by coating the inside of the joint with wood glue and screwing to the side, from the legs towards the center of the countertop, in at least four places.
- Once done, you can paint or laminate the outer sides of the island as you wish.

2) Get furniture and containers. You will need to secure various furniture and containers under the table to create usable spaces. The choice will be determined partly by the

space available, as the width of the island will determine the depth of each cabinet and partly by your needs.

- You will need to make sure that the furniture's dimensions are the same as the width and length of the table. In addition, they must not be higher than the legs.
- Use a pair of wall units with shelves and join them together to maximize usable island space. Better if the cabinets are without dividers, so you can take the items stored on both sides.

3) Secure the cabinets to the table. Screw the cabinets from the inside to secure them to the island, and screw them together if the wood is thick enough.

- Make sure you use screws that reach halfway down the wood panel. Otherwise, you risk creating cracks, deformations, or holes on the outer surface.

4) Add details and finish. You can paint the cabinets using the same color as the workbench or contrasting color. You can also tile the surface and add glulam or a granite slab.

Use a chest of drawers

1) Get a chest of drawers. If you want to turn it into a kitchen island, it needs to be the right size. With drawers that are too long or heavy, you will get a modest result. Instead, try to find something roughly the same size as the area you want to occupy.

- If you want to paint the chest of drawers, the best time to do it is now because it will be more complicated after putting the work surface in it.

2) Add legs or wheels. If the surface of the chest of drawers is too low, you can make it the desired height by adding legs (for a fixed island), wheels (to make it mobile), or using both solutions. It also evaluates the thickness of the

countertop when calculating the height of the completed island.

- The most suitable method for adding legs or wheels depends on the features of the chest of drawers. Consult an expert and follow the instructions provided with the wheels or legs.

3) Replace the back, if necessary. If the back of the dresser is ugly or damaged, replace it with a cut-to-size MDF or chipboard board. Then, carefully remove the old piece and nail the new one.

- You can make the back of the cabinet more useful by coating it with chalkboard paint - you will create a surface on which to write a grocery list with chalk or for children to play.
- Alternatively, use this space to hang hooks or bars by placing sturdy crossbars on the other side of the back panel. Finally, you can hang towels, oven mitts, or kitchen tools.

4) Replace or re-coat the countertop. To have a worktop more suitable for food preparation, you can carefully remove the top table of the cabinet and replace it with a material of your choice. It shouldn't be difficult to tile if the existing surface is smooth, with straight, finished edges. Decide what to do based on your skills, needs, and tastes.

Use kitchen cabinets

1) Buy some kitchen furniture. Any combination of kitchen cabinets that don't already have a workbench will do. In this way, you can combine them in the configuration you prefer, completing the work with the plan. In addition, you can buy furniture similar to what you already have in the kitchen, or different furniture to combine as you like.

- Pay attention to the back and sides of the furniture. If they're not finished, you'll have to do it yourself. Cover them with plywood or MDF boards which you can then paint.

2) Arrange the furniture in the order you prefer. You will probably have to join several pieces together. Do this by screwing in the furniture from the inside, using the structure areas where the wood is thickest.

- You can put furniture turned in the same direction, in opposite directions, or, if space permits, put a piece of furniture on its side. It depends on the result you are looking for and how you intend to use the space.

3) Add a surface. Once the furniture is in place, build or buy a work surface covering all the pieces. Again, you can use different materials, from glulam to granite.

Even a concrete slab (colored, patterned, or raw) can work fine. It must have dimensions suitable for your chosen furniture; make sure you leave a few extra inches in width and length for the counter's edge.

4) Do the finishes. Finally, refine the island by customizing it to your liking. You can modify it to match your style, kitchen, or home better. You can also add storage boxes to maximize work surface space, making more room for appliances or preparing fantastic family meals.

- You can paint the lower sections of your new island a contrasting color to the other furniture, or you can leave them as they are. Experiment with light shades to give it a touch pop to the kitchen, or use shades that recall the existing colors in the kitchen, such as fruit or a vase in plain sight.

- Add elements to the sides or back of the furniture. For example, you can mount a paper roll holder or hooks for kitchen rags. You can put a magazine rack for recipes or cooking magazines. You can even put a container for the kitchen tools you use most. Most of these things will need to be screwed to the wood. Always make sure to fasten them in places that are thick enough to support the screw, for example, on the shelf support or the main structure of the island. You can also use strong glues suitable for hanging items.

Take advantage of height with space organizers

Keeping the kitchen tidy is not easy; another trick is to take advantage of the height. For example, does your kitchen have doors that extend vertically? Then you have to make the most of them.

Let's say that they are not that comfortable, but you can think of inserting space organizers inside them, which you can find in specialized stores. The aforementioned will allow you to organize the kitchen better, helping you find a place for pots, lids, bowls, and objects that take up excessive space.

Organize the space by adding shelves

Another idea to avoid leaving utensils and objects around the kitchen is better organizing the space by adding shelves. The shelves represent the key elements, practical, functional, and economical, capable of helping you organize and order spaces.

1. You can think of arranging spices, bowls, cups, and small utensils on the shelves; in this way, your kitchen will be tidy, but this arrangement allows you to use the utensils as real furnishing elements. There are various types of shelves in Shabby chic, industrial, classic, modern, and Provencal styles, and you can choose the ones that best suit the style of your kitchen.
2. Use baskets and jars
3. Baskets and jars are other useful elements for ordering the kitchen. These objects are very useful for organizing the pantry to be positioned inside the doors and for organizing the worktop.
4. Jars are very useful for containing spices, rods, cereals, and baskets; on the other hand, they are perfect for legumes, vegetables, and fruit. Baskets and jars turn out to be aesthetically beautiful; you

can choose according to the style of your kitchen, but above all, they are functional and economical.

5. Prepare the doors

6. To make the most of the space, avoiding cluttering up every corner of the kitchen, you can think about setting up the doors. You can think of placing object holders on the doors, but internally. This solution is perfect, especially for the under-sink door, to contain gloves, sponges, and cleaning products; therefore, the accessories must be used frequently.

7. Arrange tools by size

8. To make the kitchen tidy, another piece of advice we can give you is to arrange the utensils in your kitchen doors according to the size. So you can think of dedicating the first shelf of your kitchen to small items such as cutlery, glasses, and bowls and the second shelf to larger items such as pots.

9. In this way, you will organize the space by grouping the elements by size, and your kitchen will be tidy and functional.

Organize by frequency of use

Another trick to ordering the kitchen is to organize not by size but by frequency of use. In this way, you will always have the objects you use most frequently at hand and those you don't use well-positioned; in this way, the order will be ensured.

Secret

The secret to always keeping the kitchen tidy is to find the aesthetic side. Ordering cups and bowls by color and creating personalized labels are brilliant ideas to make your kitchen tidy and efficient.

Tips and tricks to always keep the kitchen tidy: images and photos

We wrote this guide just for you, to help you keep the kitchen tidy. We have given you several suggestions to organize your kitchen in the best possible way to make it practical, functional, and always tidy. Now, look at these beautiful pictures.

The choice of kitchen lighting must consider different elements relating to the surrounding environment, such as the arrangement of the windows and natural light (as well as the position of the furniture), and the points to be highlighted, such as the intended floors. For example, cooking, cutting dishes, or other activities where concentration is required, both environments intended for relaxation while eating and talking with friends and relatives or family. This is made possible both by the different systems that we will choose and by the color temperature of the light that we will install in these devices, and by the color rendering index (CRI) of the LED bulbs.

This guide can be used both to give a new look to the pre-existing environments in your room and to find classic or modern design ideas for new homes still without lights or to be restored; I will try to balance the most visible design lighting sources with the more hidden ones such as kitchen chandeliers combined with recessed spotlights. Depending on the style of your environment and the point to be illuminated, you may need a point, linear, concentrated, or more diffused light source.

Made in the USA
Middletown, DE
12 May 2024

54242167R00119